New discoveries in

The Land of King Arthur

The legacy of Geoffrey of Monmouth

Stephen Clarke

With contributions by
John and Jane Bray, Peter Bere and Gordon McDonald

New discoveries in

The Land of King Arthur

The legacy of Geoffrey of Monmouth

Cover:
Fifteen hundred years of prehistoric settlements are preserved under this King's Wood Gate flood attenuation pond

Typeset, and published by Clarke Printing, Monmouth

First published 2021

ISBN 978-0-9558242-5-8

Ar gyfer fy wyrion
Ioan, Megan, Honor, Isla
my grandchildren
sydd wedi dod â llawenydd mawr

ACKNOWLEDGMENTS

Once again I am most grateful for the help and enthusiasm of Charles Boase and for the contributions from Jane and John Bray, Peter Bere, Gordon McDonald and Geoff Webb.
My son Rhodri and his partner Ellie have set and printed the manuscript and seen the book through to publication.

I also wish to thank Professor Seán McGrail, Dr Sian Rees, Ann Leaver, Martin Tuck, Dr Elizabeth Walker, Dr Mark Redknap, Neil Reese, Reg Clarke, Mark Lodwick, Professor Francesco Menotti, Dr Neil Phillips and Adam, Sue and the late David Harrison, Phil Riches and the Dean Group, the management and workmen of Barratt Homes, David Wilson Homes and Siltbusters on the King's Wood Gate site and the management and workmen of Charles Church (Parc Glyndŵr) and of course my long-suffering wife, Hazel.

No book on Early Medieval Monmouth would be complete without the acknowledgement of the research and publications of Dave Hancocks - another Monmouth boy who was schooled alongside the shade of Geoffrey of Monmouth in Priory Street. Keep it up Dave!

CONTENTS

Left: A 5th or 6th century Anglo-Saxon silver sword jewel, from soil on the floor of the pre-Norman building at 22-24 Monnow Street. Before conservation.

Right: A 5th or 6th century Anglo-Saxon gold sword jewel after conservation from the Sutton Hoo burial.

Radiocarbon dates are given as 'years BP',
meaning 'years before present'.

The benchmark date for 'present' is 1950.

Some of the text has been repeated from earlier editions
to put more recent discoveries into context.

ILLUSTRATIONS

WE HAVE called this book *Discoveries in the Land of King Arthur* in recognition of Geoffrey of Monmouth who took the name of our town and made it famous around the world. Geoffrey's contribution towards how the British and even to some extent, how the Europeans see themselves, is captivating, although we may have forgotten why. Ours is King Arthur country where the hills and valleys seem to some of us ring with Arthurian echoes.

There are two stories in this book involving the mythical King which were centred on Monmouth and were inspired by the prehistoric lake which once filled the great bowl which is now the site of the town. They feature in some of the famous stories of Sir Mortimer Wheeler's 'indubitable Arthur' and scores of other literary works such as T.H. White's *Once and Future King*.

The famous Mabinogion tale of the hunting of the evil boar, Twrch Trwyth, from Ireland to Cornwall, via Monmouth, like Geoffrey's tidal Monmouth and the millstones on the shore of the lake, identify Monmouth's lake as the enchanted lake of Llyn Lliwan.

Nennius, in the 9th century, and Geoffrey of Monmouth, in the 12th century, tell of a tidal Monmouth as one of Nennius' Wonders of Britain. With the rising tide, joined by the waters of the three rivers and the accumulated detritus, a 'mountain' of water was released down the Wye Valley at the turning of the tide. There is archaeological and geological evidence that this story is a true record of a natural phenomenon in Monmouth.

In Monmouth we have our own link to the great archaeologists of the past via A. L. Sockett, our Society's late president, who had dug with Kathleen Kenyon, excavator of Jericho. 'Sox' organised our first archaeological excavation under the apple trees behind St James' House in 1956 where three young schoolboys were welcomed to learn and practise the 'Wheeler School' of archaeology.

Archaeology has always attracted controversy, for the subject lends itself to differing interpretations which can quickly inspire disputes. American anthropology has been even more exciting, especially during early modem times when fossil hunters carried guns – and would use them too, given the opportunity. Surely, we have all been wrong in advocating some theory or other, but being reluctant to correct ourselves can compound the error and rather raise the temperature. Over the years I have seen many disagreements including, of course, some caused by myself, and am tempted to present a few of them here; however, I will give just one example, especially as it has an Arthurian element.

We dug for ten years under the shops at Nos 22-24 Monnow Street where just about every historical period was represented and where there was a layer of 'sterile' soil between the Roman contexts and the medieval ones. We decided that it was plough soil and the equivalent of the 'Dark Earth over many Roman towns, it occurs on many of the sites in Monmouth. On the street frontage of 24 Monnow Street, a row of large post-holes, marking a very substantial structure, had been cut through the 'plough soil' into the underlying levels where only Roman and earlier remains were found, including Roman and Iron Age pottery and buildings constructed on sleeper beams. The stratification was clear and was supported by 11th century pottery, and later by coin and archaeomagnetic dating. This meant that we had fairly certainly unearthed the remains of a pre-Norman structure which, with the archaeology, was a highly significant discovery, especially in a border town between England and Wales – for long, contested country. I contacted several archaeologists who I thought would be interested, including some from the National Museum of Wales and the University of Wales. So several of us gathered on the site where I presented our interpretation of the remains and stressed their significance. All was amicable, even when I had finished and the University specialist in early medieval archaeology, said: "I don't believe it!" I asked what was wrong as the evidence, supported by the stratification, was manifest and could only be interpreted as the remains being pre-Norman. He simply repeated: "But I don't believe it." And that's where the matter rested.

The discovery which would surely have settled the debate on the site occurred later – when we found a 6th or early 7th-century Anglo-Saxon sword stud in soil from the floor of the structure. This was the first sword stud of its type to be found in Wales or the West and was a remarkable discovery.

By now there was a proposal to demolish No 20, next door, which obviously threatened the archaeology there and that associated with the Early Medieval building; it also threatened the Norman town defences which crossed the site on their way from Monmouth Castle to the River Wye. Also, we had discovered the front defences of

Monmouth's Pre-Flavian Roman Fort in the garden to the rear of the building. Since that time Anglo-Saxon pottery has come from three sites in the town including a sherd of Chester Ware recovered by the Glamorgan-Gwent Archaeological Trust on the Kwiksave site (83-85 Monnow Street); all are known to be pre-Norman.

I thought that the sword jewel would help to safeguard No 20, from redevelopment. The shop was deteriorating and was now said to be becoming unsafe – a potential repeat of the precursor to the illegal demolition of the Georgian Kwiksave building and the consequent truly disastrous groundworks which destroyed the archaeology during re-building. A Cadw-funded archaeological excavation of a single trench failed to reach the Norman levels although the sherd of Anglo-Saxon Chester Ware was found, but unstratified. The head of medieval studies at the National Museum of Wales had identified the sword stud which was matched by two gold ones from the royal burial at Sutton Hoo in East Anglia. It was a highly important discovery and we began our campaign by publicising the danger to the site if the shop should be demolished.

The Press gave us good coverage, the Western Mail and Western Daily Press devoting full pages to the story. However, the campaign was damaged when the newspapers printed a statement from the Senior Historic Environment Officer of the Glamorgan-Gwent Archaeological Trust. The report of the National Museum's identification of the stud was followed by:

> *But the Glamorgan-Gwent Archaeological Trust's specialist advisor to Monmouthshire County Council was less certain of the find's significance: 'We know very little in reality about what was happening in Wales between the Romans and the Normans,' he said. 'We have lots of legends and stories but very little in the way of absolute fact and archaeological record. It's possible that what we've got with this find is evidence of the Normans arriving.* It's also possible it's earlier but the Anglo-Saxon stud doesn't prove that. All we can say for certain is that there was activity there at the Normans' time, which is still hugely significant.'*
>
> WalesOnline 6.6.2009/accessed 28 MAR 2013)

*Of course the Normans did arrive in Monmouth – but five hundred years later!

Author's Note

I HAVE been digging in Monmouth for over sixty years, which inspired one of the young ladies in our team to comment: "So it's about time that you found something!" Actually I think that she really meant something 'shiny'. However, the group has been fairly successful otherwise – with a handful of Roman forts, a medieval town, Stone Age settlements, first medieval and post-medieval pottery and tile kilns, six feet of intact medieval house floors along Monnow Street, hunter-gatherer camp sites and Bronze Age settlements with buildings on stilts together with a unique collection of 5,000-year-old worked timbers resembling parts of a Stone Age boat.

When, in September 1986, we first encountered the remarkable archaeology under Monnow Street, it seemed as though all else had led up to that moment. It did, in fact, lead to winning the Silver Trowel and the Pitt-Rivers awards but now we find that there are far older remains under our town than we knew, so once again it seems as though all else has led up to this time.

This book describes the discoveries made in and around the site of the post-glacial lake in the bowl of Monmouth; it also shows that the Lake was the one which inspired the myth of Llyn Lliwan – the magic lake which features in the earliest prose literature of Wales and the story of King Arthur in the saga of Culhwch and Olwen. The evidence for this is threefold: firstly, the route of the famous hunting of the boar, Twrch Trwyth, which was said to have been led by King Arthur, across Wales to Ewyas in northern Gwent and down to the mouth of the Wye at Chepstow – passing the Monmouth Lake.

Secondly, there is solid archaeological evidence that an incident said to have taken place in the southern waters of Llyn Lliwan could only have been imagined as being at Monmouth.

Thirdly, there is archaeological proof that the tidal incursions into Llyn Lliwan and the subsequent 'Wonder of Britain' outbursts of water recorded by the monks, Nennius and Geoffrey of

Monmouth, in the 9th and 12th centuries, did in fact take place and that the monks were probably eye witnesses from Monmouth Priory.

When one of my friends heard that we had archaeological evidence that an Arthurian story in the Mabinogion was a true record of an ancient event and had been inspired by sites in Monmouth, his instant reaction was "Don't touch it!" Of course he had a point, for tales of King Arthur and the writings of his champion, Geoffrey of Monmouth, are usually seen as pure mythology and have caused considerable damage to some reputations, especially to that of John Morris for his *magnum opus 'The Age of Arthur'*. In this first inspired attempt to bring history and archaeology of the early medieval period together Morris treats Arthur as a real person with real events. However, despite the growing evidence for the existence of the great Dark Age leader, even referring to something as 'Arthurian' can be risky. But King Arthur does appear to have been a real person – and he sells books. And as for the whole lot being fiction, I can do no better than quote Sir Mortimer Wheeler in his introduction to Leslie Alcock's 1972 book, '*By South Cadbury, is that Camelot . . .*'

> *"Then there is now at last an indubitable 'Arthur' or his ilk. And, five centuries after his shadowy but persistent shape had on any showing passed from the scene, late Saxon kings seemingly struck coins there and surrounded their mint with a solid mortared wall. In half-a-dozen directions the site has offered rich rewards to Alcock and his colleagues, and has incidentally made kindly nonsense of those earnest scholars who, desperately anxious to preserve their scientific integrity from Arthurian pollution, hesitated to approve a serious venture amidst the half-memories which are happily an occasional and often decorative part of historic humanism. Let these young critics, bless them, in this sort of context recall the epic battles and victories of Troy long ago, and of a certain Heinrich Schliemann who was not afraid so to venture . . ."*
>
> *MORTIMER WHEELER*

"those earnest scholars who, desperately anxious to preserve their scientific integrity from Arthurian pollution, . . ."

Obviously it does not concern us!

Where three rivers meet –
At the post-glacial lake of Llyn Lliwan

(From 'The Lost Lake', 2016)

The Livox, where Llyn Lliwan drained into the Wye Valley

THE counties of Hereford, Gloucester and Monmouth meet in the Wye gorge to the east of Monmouth where the river is overlooked by limestone cliffs, prehistoric cave dwellings, and the great Iron Age hill fort of the Little Doward. Here, as you cross the border into Wales, the valley suddenly opens to reveal a panoramic bowl edged by wooded hills with Monmouth set on rising ground, above where three rivers meet. The Wye, the Monnow and the Troddi are some of the most beautiful rivers in the world but as they pass serenely around the town we forget their occasional dramatic and devastating floods. Rivers were higher during various prehistoric times when sea levels were raised, while much later, Monmouth town was a place where ocean-going boats were built and launched to faraway seas – that was during the 19th century when one of the last *(The Monmouth)* overturned – with the Mayor and Corporation on board.

Today, it would come as a shock to most people standing to admire our famous medieval bridge to realise that almost into historical times they would have been under water – for the Monmouth basin had once been filled by one of the largest of prehistoric lakes in Wales (*The Lost Lake*).

It might also come as a shock to hear that, in the 9th century, during the time of the monk Nennius and in the 12th century, during the life of Geoffrey of Monmouth, the town was tidal. These two monks describe tidal inundations into the Monmouth Lake (we now believe was the magic lake of Llyn Lliwan) and the subsequent huge outburst of water from the three rivers with the ebb tide. These stories are supported by archaeology for a layer of estuarine clay, deposited by the tides, survives around the shores of the ancient lake.

Prehistoric activities beside and overlooking the lake which we have discovered in Monmouth town began with the camp sites of Middle Stone Age hunter-gatherers some 6,000 to 8,000 years ago. There is also evidence of a 5,000-year-old crannog in the lake which may be associated with timbers resembling parts of a Neolithic boat bearing strange cuts and worn features with five radiocarbon dates centred on 5,000 years BP (before 'the present', 1950).

There are also the remains of New Stone Age to Bronze Age lake settlements with buildings on stilts in and beside the lake.

After much of the lake had been drained there was a Roman iron-working industry and possibly a Roman vineyard on the former bed of the lake.

The setting of the Monmouth Lake

MONMOUTH lies in a natural bowl which geologists say was cut by the action of glacial ice arriving down the Monnow Valley from the north and the Troddi Valley from the west and possibly joined by ice coming down the Wye Valley too. The ice accumulated at the junction of the three valleys where its exit was impeded by the narrow Wye gorge immediately below Monmouth so that it ground out the great hollow in which the town sits today. It is believed that at the end of the Ice Age the gorge may have been partially blocked by detritus brought down with meltwater and a large fresh-water lake formed in the 'bowl' (Searle, E.J., 1970).

What evidence is there for the Monmouth Lake and how long did it exist? Today, we believe we have learnt a lot more about the lake and its environs and we can with some confidence suggest the phases in the life of the lake and even draw some conclusions about how it came to disappear.

During the most remote times Monmouth would have been the site of an ice lake where ice had gathered in the bowl filling the lower parts of Monmouth leaving Gibraltar Hill standing like a large island in the lake. At the end of the Ice Ages with the melting of the ice sheets and the consequent blocking of the valley – probably somewhere in the lower Wyesham area – the first fresh-water lake, was formed – as described by Elsa Searle in 1970. This would have been a huge volume of water which may have spread up the local valleys. How deep the lake would have been on the site of the future town we may never know for sure – perhaps the geologists may be able to find out – but it would almost certainly have covered the future town up to the Priory Church and extended some way up the surrounding valleys. One can get some idea of the quantity of water from looking out across Vauxhall from Priory Street and imagining the lake reaching to your feet when the ice sheets had retreated with melt-water extending out across the meadow into the distance (see p78).

With the arrival of humans around the lake most of the pre-Ice Age archaeology had been washed away – with the exception of the fossils preserved in refuges like King Arthur's Cave on the Great Doward or perhaps in the hillside fields above the glacial outwash. There are a few Palaeolithic style flints from the Trellech highlands and the single Old Stone Age hand-axe found by Bob Flynn in the plough soil at Welsh Newton, but otherwise the evidence is meagre indeed.

The first intrepid 'hunter-gatherers' set up their camps overlooking the lake in what was to become St James' Street and Wyebridge Street. The distinctive Middle Stone Age microliths from the harpoons of the hunters in St James' Street were preserved in the fine sandy soil which also contained a late Iron Age potsherd supported by two radiocarbon dates from charcoal and bone. The deposit was then covered with a thick layer of graded pebbles and sand seemingly carried down by a sort of 'storm-rush' down the Wye Valley to the site. The layer was deposited during the late Iron Age or around the time of the arrival of the Romans in the First Century AD. After that the peat built up all around that area of Overmonnow – from Wonastow Road to the Croft-y-Bwla side of Parc Glyndŵr and this may mark the edge of the final fresh-water lake with the depth of the water increasing towards the east, to beyond Jordan Way.

Estimating the time for the growth of the peat is complicated but it may have been just a few millimetres a year overall although it appears to have happened fairly quickly in Monmouth and was probably closely linked to the draining of the lake. The peat sealed the earlier pondweed marl on the bed of the lake at Parc Glyndŵr which, incidentally, was not found on the Barratt Homes site. The peat also filled the channels which were unearthed during the APAC excavations in the Barratt's attenuation pond (one containing a sealed Roman coin).

The radiocarbon dates point to a long series of occupations and activities in and around the lake while the peat may indicate the extent of the lake during its final phase. During a period in the later

Bronze Age there appears to have been lower water levels which left slightly higher ground exposed around the valleys. Such open areas were subjected to wet/dry, wet/dry conditions which caused the decay of most organic remains except for a few large prehistoric tree stumps with rotted surfaces and rotted inner cores. There was very little in the way of plant remains preserved under the peat lower down the site – except for the occasional well-rotted tree bole.

After a large part of the lake had drained, activities on the old lake bed included a Roman iron-working site and a possible Roman vineyard (the very much earlier remains were found in St James' Street and upper Monnow Street). During medieval and post-medieval times settlements had often moved to the higher ground while later there was a concentrated attempt to drain the site of the lake – but with limited success. That is now being followed by extensive modern housing developments using large flood attenuation ponds and deep, complex drainage systems.

It seems that it was during Roman and early medieval times that Llyn Lliwan slowly silted up and, with the slightly lower sea levels, eventually faded into myth and legend although some Monmouth farmers appear to have kept alive a rather misty memory of the pebbly shores of the lost Lake.

Now sea levels are rising again.

A lot was happening in and around the lake 5,000 years ago. Indeed, one of the upright posts set in the lake bed has been dated to 6,000 years ago. The forest below the mouth of the River Troddi on the Welsh bank of the Wye, where the river bends at the very start of the lower Wye gorge, is called the 'Livox Wood'. This may be derived from the Welsh Llif–from Llifeiriog – 'flow' or 'overflow' (linked to Llifddwrfr – flood and Llifeiriant – flood, deluge or current) this may be related to the edge of the lake or its drainage and the sometimes tidal water. The name Llyn is of course Welsh for Lake but Lliwan is unclear. There is another 'Livox' in the lower Wye Valley above Chepstow.

Some of the Prehistoric Discoveries on the Overmonnow Flood plain – radiocarbon dates are BP – before the present (1950).

The King's Wood Gate is in green,
Parc Glyndŵr is in yellow.

Jane Bray

House foundations on the site of the Monmouth Lake

Typical house foundations into the site of the bed of Llyn Lliwan

Llyn Lliwan – The Lost Lake and a 9th Century 'Wonder of Britain'

THE MABINOGION story of Culhwch and Olwen, featuring the mythical lake of Llyn Lliwan, is the earliest folk tale of King Arthur and his knights where the lake was said to be the home of the oldest living creature on earth – the magic salmon of Llyn Lliwan.

The salmon of Llyn Lliwan? By a Monmouth potter in cAD1240

In the 14th century the story of the lake was immortalised as one of the tales forming the Mabinogion – translated from two medieval Middle Welsh books (the White Book of Rhydderch, c.1325 and the Red Book of Hergest c.1400) by Lady Charlotte Guest. The stories are from earlier oral traditions.

It was always thought that the story of the lake was based on a real lake, situated somewhere in south-east Wales and recorded by monks in the 9th and 12th centuries before being used in the 14th century Mabinogion. But as there was no lake known in the region, historians speculated that the inspiration for the story lay elsewhere and they produced an array of suggested sites, including The Whirly Holes of Caldicot, Caerwent, the Neddern Valley, the mouth of the Usk and probably the strangest of all, but still popular amongst academics, a 'tidal lake,' whatever that was, in the Severn.

However, if the antiquaries who studied the story had known that there had been an ancient lake in Monmouth and if they had followed the route of the legendary boar hunt across Wales and down the Monnow Valley, on the way to the mouth of the Wye, as described in the story, they would have arrived at the site of the lake. The Monmouth Lake attracted continuous settlement for many thousands of years and has produced some of the earliest prehistoric remains in Wales. Also, a bizarre incident in the story, which was said to have taken place on the southern side of the lake, gives the ultimate credence to the belief that the site of the mythical lake has finally been recognised.

The medieval descriptions of Llyn Lliwan by Nennius and Geoffrey of Monmouth concerning the tidal in-flow and out-flow of Llyn Lliwan appear to have been first-hand accounts (at least for Nennius). Their records (page 27) are dramatically supported by the archaeological evidence of what was happening on the ground at the time – the essential evidence being the layer of 'estuarine' type of clay laid down by the tides around the shores of the lake apparently in medieval times.

The Discovery

MONMOUTH archaeologists have been working on building sites, roadworks and pastureland in and around the town since the 1950s – much of the time as 'rescue' archaeologists on threatened remains. Although geologists had said that there had been a post-glacial lake in the Monmouth bowl and there was clearly an ancient alluvial 'natural' base to the land around the town we did not realise that we were actually on what was until comparatively recently the bed and shore of the prehistoric lake.

Elsa Searle, a Geography teacher at St Julians High School in Newport, produced a study of the rivers of Monmouthshire in 1970. Her work includes a study of the geology of the Monmouth basin and sets the background scene to the prehistoric lake and the more recent archaeological discoveries made by Monmouth archaeologists in and around it over the last few years (Searle, E.: *The Rivers of Monmouthshire*, 1970 and Clarke, S.: *The Lost Lake*, 2016).

An early Bronze Age enigma

THERE had been clues – one of the best being an unusually small early Bronze Age barbed and tanged flint arrowhead which was very water-worn and which came from the 'natural' gravels and pebbles at 24 Monnow Street – high above the modern rivers and, as we thought at the time, well above the waters of any lake. However, it must have been polished by the gentle lapping of the water along the shoreline – as can be seen around Llangors and other lakes.

24 Monnow Street. This water-worn early Bronze Age arrowhead came from the ancient alluvial gravels, high above the modern rivers, but apparently on the edge of the Monmouth post-glacial lake. Scale: 1 cm

Just as surprising was the discovery of two hunter-gatherers' camp sites overlooking the southern side of the lake in St. James' Street and Wyebridge Street. We had often found microliths, the small flint barbs from harpoons, in the surface of the 'natural' in Monnow Street while the Roman occupation levels often lay directly upon the natural, so perhaps we should have asked if they were there when the lake was first drained.

Elsa Searle's book was followed by the building of new housing estates around Monmouth which revealed a proliferation of remains on the flood plains and shores of the lake – these were dated from the Middle Stone Age to Roman times but especially from the Bronze Age – usually beside the site of the lake but also sometimes in it.

The St James' Street gas mains section: The dark layer of iron slag in the middle of the section was Roman and lay directly above the pebbles and sand of the alluvial deposit which itself seals the sand at the bottom of the section. The worked flints and other finds from the Mesolithic camp site came from the sand layer at the bottom of the section as did a sherd of late Iron Age pottery and two associated First Century radiocarbon dates.

From 'The Lost Lake'. Photograph: Denis Loffhagen

Rescuing a 5,000-year-old structural oak stilt in the bed of the lake

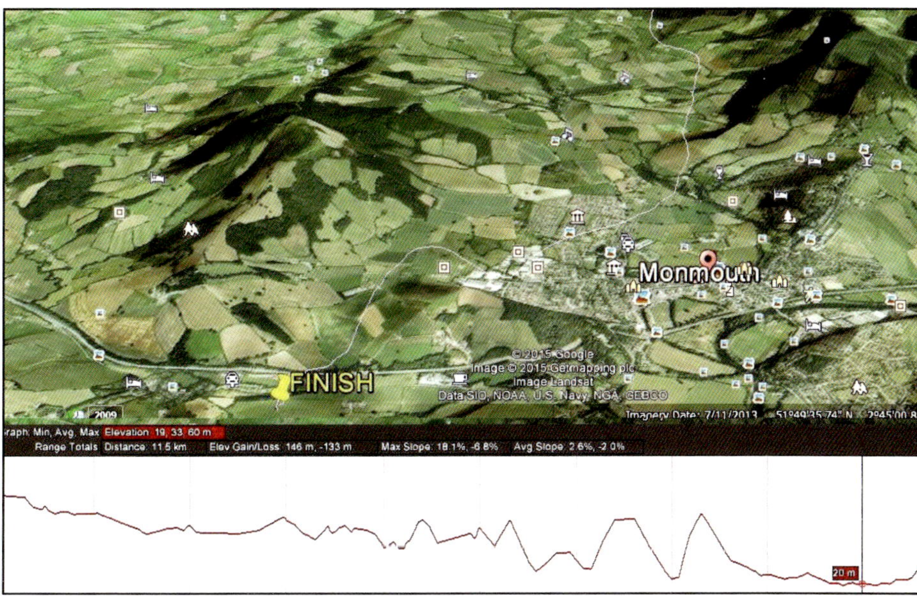

Peter Bere's section though the bowl of Monmouth

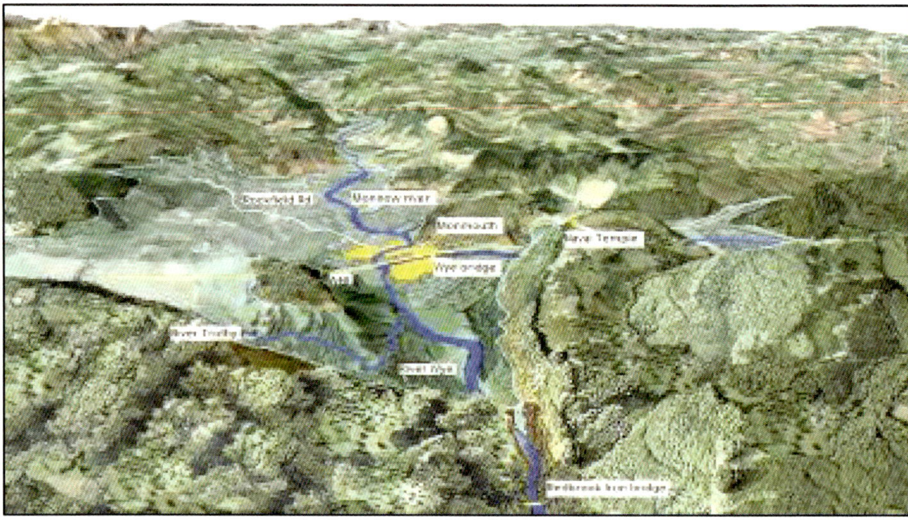

Peter Bere's Google map reconstruction of the Monmouth Lake:
One million to 10,000 years ago.

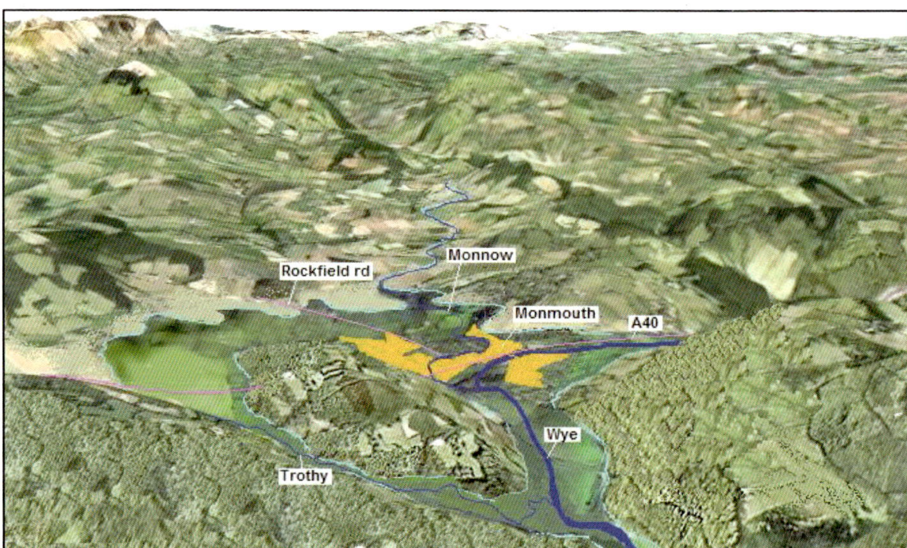

Peter Bere's Google map reconstruction of the Monmouth Lake:
Holocene, 9,000 to 2,500 years ago.

St James' Street. The lake shore of graded pebbles and sand covering the silty sand which produced the Middle Stone Age remains and the First Century radiocarbon dates, together with a late Iron Age potsherd. Photograph: Denis Loffhagen

There was a very similar Middle Stone Age camp site, with microliths, on the surface of the natural to the west, in nearby Wye Bridge Street which would also have been overlooking the lake.

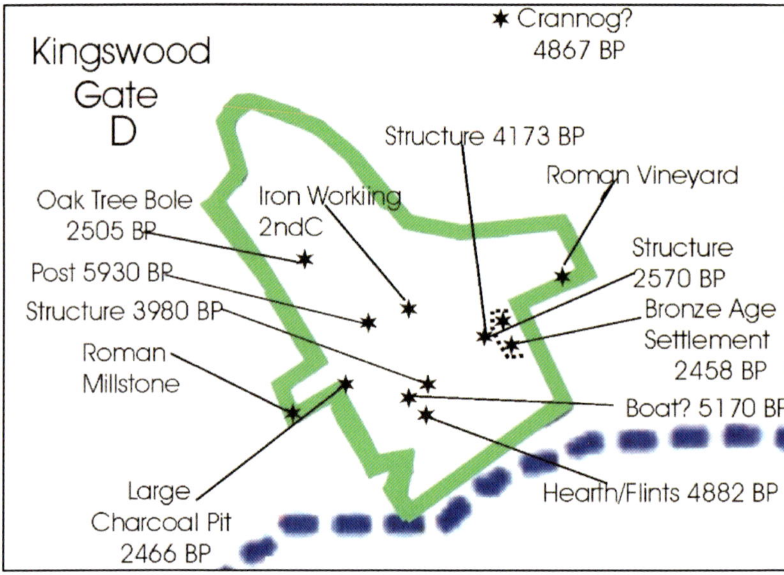

Recent discoveries at King's Wood – dates before 1950. Jane Bray

Monmouth Archaeology (thc professional wing of Monmouth Archaeological Society) were the archaeological contractors for Barratt Homes and for David Wilson Homes during the building of the new estates off Wonastow Road, Overmonnow. The unit was also the contractor for Siltbusters during their adjoining industrial development and was previously the contractor for Charles Church at Parc Glyndŵr – all very archaeologically rich and informative sites.

Five hundred houses have been completed off Wonastow Road, together with a large industrial building (Siltbusters) on land which was once the bed and shore of the prehistoric lake filling the bowl of Monmouth.

Both developments now have large attenuation ponds in place to control flood waters and both are now preserving a range of settlements covering many thousands of years – especially some of the Bronze Age and the New Stone Age.

Barratt's housing development at King's Wood Gate, Overmonnow.

Drainage excavations into the bed of the lake, revealing the post-glacial story of the fresh water lake (thin white clay) followed by the silting of the lake, followed by the growth of peat, under a layer of alluvial clay, capped by medieval and later humus.

In the background, to the west, is the White Hill with several Roman forts on its left shoulder.

There are also the sites of four medieval to post-medieval farms under the leaf mould of the woods on the hill. A fifth ancient farm has been converted into a dwelling.

Barratt's King's Wood Gate, drainage section through the lake bed

Barratt's King's Wood Gate, Roman iron-working site

The magic lake of Llyn Lliwan

Llyn Lliwan – where the Monnow joins the rivers Wye and Troddi (Peter Bere)

THE Lake of Llyn Lliwan is first recorded in the 9th century, apparently by the monk Nennius – as one of the Wonders of Britain. It is described as being a lake up a river with the river mouth flowing into the Severn – like the Monmouth Lake: *'There is another wonder: it is the confluence of Linn Liuan; the mouth of that river flows into the Severn . . .'* the 'flood' is received into the lake and with the ebbing of the tide the lake 'vomits all that it has devoured. And in a likeness of a mountain in one wave it spews and bursts'. Llyn Lliwan is mentioned in similar vein by Geoffrey of Monmouth, the 12th century author of the *History of the Kings of Britain,* which established King Arthur as a mythological world-renowned hero. Geoffrey says that Llyn Lliwan was 'near the Severn' – not in it – and records the same outburst of the water.

This is surely a description of a lake fed by several rivers (and backed up by the tide, which, it is worth repeating (page 33), is still recognisable in Monmouth town) and which then runs into the River Wye. It then joins the Severn which fits the circumstances and the description of the two monks far more convincingly than the now traditional hypothetical tidal lake in the estuary.

When I first saw the light-coloured 'anaerobic' alluvial clay in the trench around Parc Glyndŵr I immediately thought that it was estuarine but could not imagine the sea reaching as far inland as the countryside around Monmouth; also, the deposit appeared to be reasonably recent. However, both of the medieval monks – Nennius and Geoffrey of Monmouth – speak of the tide filling or topping up the lake of Llyn Lliwan – *'receiving it* (the water) *into the lake in the mode of a whirlpool*'. And at the ebbing of the tide bursting out and '*vomiting all that it has devoured in the likeness of a mountain in one wave it spews and bursts'.*

I am grateful to Peter Bere for pointing out that even today the 'slack water' reaches up to and beyond Wye Bridge (see the 19th and 20th century photographs on page 34). If the sea level had been a little higher (it was when boats could reach the walls of Caerwent in Roman times and large ocean-going boats were built in Monmouth and launched into the River Wye downstream of the bridge) in the 19th century. In the Middle Ages the tide would have held back more of the fresh water from the three rivers so that with the 'slack water' there would have been a considerable accumulation which could flow across the Overmonnow flood plain (and create a copy of Llyn Lliwan?).

Both Nennius and Geoffrey of Monmouth (some think that Geoffrey was copying Nennius) describe Llyn Lliwan as being a lake on a river with a 'Teared' – 'tear'or 'break'? – which may refer to the Wye dividing into the three rivers at the Monmouth lake.

We are now convinced that the Monmouth Lake was the original Llyn Lliwan and that medieval tides explain the anaerobic or alluvial clay layer over the peat phase which so resembles the shining brown mud that can be seen along the banks of the Wye at Chepstow. The clay fills many of the prehistoric and later archaeological features across the two developments at Overmonnow and must be related to the marshy fields of the low ground from Parc Glyndŵr to the land below Croft-y-Bwla.

There was also the indication that the clay, being just below the topsoil, was not really very ancient. Also, we had a Roman radiocarbon date from the peat under the clay and a 2nd century sherd of Samian Ware sealed between two layers of the clay. There was also a Roman coin from inside the peat which filled one of the channels excavated by APAC in the Barratt's attenuation pond.

So it appears to me to be certain that the clay was laid down during Roman times, continuing into the Middle Ages when the medieval warm period is said to have been from around AD950 to AD1250. And sea levels would probably then have been rather different. This would have been during the lives of the two monks, so it could well be that the monks themselves had first-hand experience of Llyn Lliwan and the behaviour of the lake.

Geoffrey of Monmouth seems to have spent a lot of his time in Oxford – which was probably where he wrote his world famous book on the History of Britain which featured King Arthur and the Knights of the Round Table.

Geoffrey was clearly quite proud of his Welsh and Monmouth origins and if he had looked through a window of Monmouth Priory he would have seen the Llyn Lliwan Lake and its activities for himself. That may have been exactly what he did for the Priory overlooked the Overmonnow part of the lake where the inflow and outflow of the lake would have been clearly visible and is where the most striking archaeological record of the tidal inundations was has been preserved in the ground.

Siltbusters attenuation pond – the 'anaerobic' clay covers the peat

'Estuarine' clay filling prehistoric features at Parc Glyndŵr

King's Wood Gate builders' drainage excavation showing anaerobic estuarine type of clay over Roman or later peat which covers the off-white lime marl which was produced by fresh-water pondweed

Parc Glyndŵr: A Bronze Age burnt mound cut by three prehistoric channels which were filled with anaerobic alluvial clay

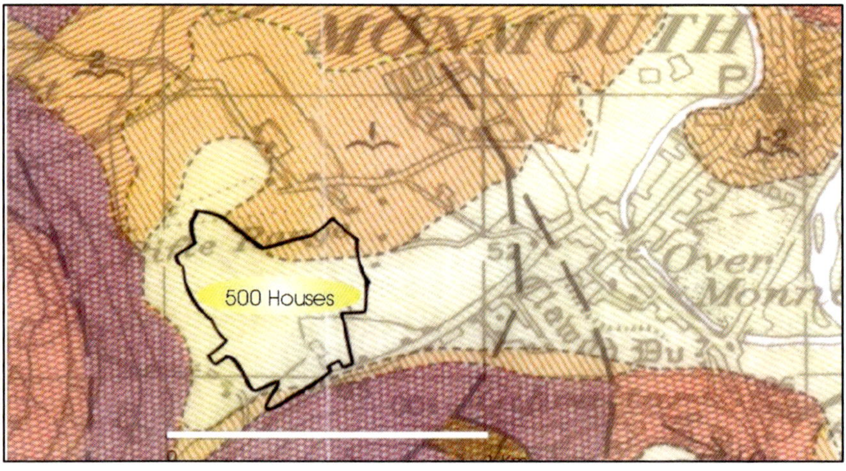

400 new houses were planned on the Alluvium but 500 were built. Other developers have bought fields on the flood plain to the north.

Nennius and Geoffrey – The documents

Nennius: *'There is another wonder: it is the confluence of Linn Liuan; the mouth of that river flows into the Severn, and when both the Severn is flooded to The Teared [?]. And the sea is flooded similarly into the aforementioned mouth of the river, both it is received into the lake/pool of the mouth in the mode of a whirlpool and the sea does not advance up. And a bank/shore exists near the river, and so long as the Severn is flooded to The Teared [?] that bank/shore is not covered, and when the sea and Severn ebbs, at that time lake Liuan vomits all that it has devoured from the sea and both that bank/shore is covered and in the likeness of a mountain in one wave it spews and bursts. And if there was the army of the whole region, in the midst of where it is, and it directed its face against the wave, even the army the wave carries off through the force, by fluid full clothes. If, on the other hand, the backs of the army were turned against it, the same wave doesn't harm, and when the sea may have ebbed, then the entire bank, which the wave covers, backwards is bared and the sea recedes from it.'*

Nennius, Historia Brittonum. LXXIII (*Operlin Livan*, the mouth of the pond of Liwan); on the forms of this name, see Sir John Rhys, *The Arthurian Legend,* p. 360,

Geoffrey of Monmouth: *'He told him likewise of another pond in Wales, near the Severn, called by the country people Linligwan, into which when the sea flows, it receives it in the manner of a gulf, but so as to swallow up the tide, and never be filled, or have its banks covered by it. But at the ebbing of the sea, it throws out the waters which it had swallowed, as high as a mountain, and at last dashes and covers the banks with them. In the meantime, if all the people of that country should stand near with their faces towards it, and happened to have their clothes sprinkled with the dashing of the waves, they would hardly, if at all, escape being swallowed up by the pond. But with their backs towards it, they need not fear being dashed, though they stood upon the very banks.'*
Geoffrey of Monmouth, Historia Regum Britanniae (History of the Kings of Britain).

Autumn mists – recreating the mythical lake of Llyn Lliwan

THE discovery of the site of an ancient lake at Monmouth answers questions that archaeologists and historians have been puzzling over ever since Lady Charlotte Guest translated the stories of the Mabinogion in the 19th century – especially where was the inspiration for the magic lake called Llyn Lliwan? A lake of that name was recorded in the 9th century by the monk Nennius and in the 12th century by Geoffrey of Monmouth. Their descriptions were of a lake topped up by the tide, on a river which fed into the Severn, this fits the Monmouth Lake and its archaeology while the Mabinogion story provides clear details of the location of the lake at Monmouth.

The tales of the two monks tell of tidal inundations into the lake and of the subsequent outbursts with the ebbing of the tide. These fit the archaeological record where the tides have left a layer of 'estuarine' clay. The peat of the lake has been dated, by coin, pottery and radiocarbon evidence, to the Roman period and perhaps later.

'Estuarine' clay laid down over Roman-phase peat by tides (all pre-dated by fresh-water pondweed white marl at the bottom left)

Parc Glyndŵr: The floodplain marshland before development

'Estuarine' alluvial clay left by tides over peat around the Monmouth Lake with the white pondweed marl just showing through the peat

17th Century map of Wales by Humphrey Lhuyd apparently showing the coast (and the tide?) extending up the Wye Valley to Monmouth

Excavations into the bed of the Monmouth Lake with estuarine' clay (at c 0.5m) deposited by post-Roman and medieval tides

The stratification (from the bottom up):
1. White lime marl at the bottom of the trench – produced by Potamogeton pondweed in the fresh-water lake.
2. Peat (black) – radiocarbon date of 176-212 cal BC 1755 ± 30 BC).
3. Light brown/off white – Estuarine clay from the medieval tidal incursions recorded by Nennius and Geoffrey of Monmouth in the 9th and 12th centuries.
4. Brown at the top – Humus from the estuarine clay and topsoil mix.

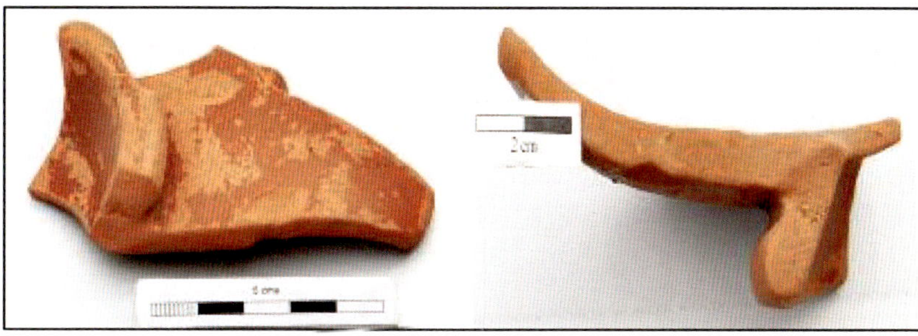

Second-century Roman Samian Ware sealed in the 'estuarine type clay' at Parc Glyndŵr

The Llyn Lliwan vortex and the tide at Monmouth

THE dramatic 'whirlpool' and other happenings in the Llyn Lliwan story can be interpreted as the result of tides backing up the River Wye to join the lake at the 'break'? of the Wye into three rivers (the 'Teared'?) and the release of the accumulated water at the turning of the tide. The resulting outflow would have been considerable and impressive, with floating debris and water movements and whirlpools as sometimes seen in the flood waters of the Severn and the Wye today. This explanation is something similar to the Bromwich and Evans idea that the Wonder referred to the spated River Usk causing a whirlpool on meeting the River Severn (Bromwich and Evans, 1992).

Although not now tidal, the rise and fall of the tides is still detectable in Monmouth town – as a shade of its past links to the estuary – and this has been properly recorded by Peter Bere (associated with the Wye River Board) and can sometimes be seen from Monmouth Quay and the Wye Bridge (p 34).

The early descriptions of the lake attributed to the 9th century Nennius and Geoffrey of Monmouth in the 12th century, describe Llyn Lliwan as being a lake on a river which runs into the Severn.

Both of the medieval passages have to be describing the Monmouth rivers backing up before the incoming tide and reaching the lake and parts of the flood plain around the town. The anaerobic clay, which extends across much of the site of the lake, must have been deposited by the tides during the Middle Ages: areas that today are being developed as housing estates.

So the archaeological evidence that the Monmouth Lake was at one time topped up by the tide is strangely confirmed by the ghost of the tide at Monmouth today. Also of course it is known that water in the estuary reached the walls of Caerwent and Caerleon. The rivers themselves would have built up in front of the tides and with their help at the turning of the tide a great wave would have been launched down the valley.

Tidal effect: Still water in the 19th century River Wye at Monmouth – thought to have been held back by the tides in the lower Wye Valley.

20th century still water beside Monmouth's Wye Bridge, thought to be caused by a high tide in the lower Wye Valley.

The tides would gather floating timber and other detritus (I've seen dead sheep and Graham Symonds of the Monmouth Canoe Centre has even witnessed a large oak tree and a dead wild boar floating *upstream* at Whitebrook). At the turning of the tide there would have been a rush of water and a 'spewing' out of the flotsam it had 'swallowed' – as described by the two medieval monks.

It was not until we recognised the slack water for what it was that the possibility that the tide itself may not necessarily have needed to reach into Overmonnow – although the anaerobic 'estuarine' type of clay appears to show that it did. As Gordon McDonald says, it could be that the tide itself laid down the estuarine clay more effectively than the slack water would have done – as on the banks of rivers joining the Severn Estuary.

The clay breaks down into muddy water but re-forms as a solid beneath slow-moving or stationary water along the shores of the lake. It would have naturally filled the hollows and archaeological features above the peat of the flood plain.

Peter Bere's reconstruction of post-medieval life on the banks of the River Wye near Wye Bridge

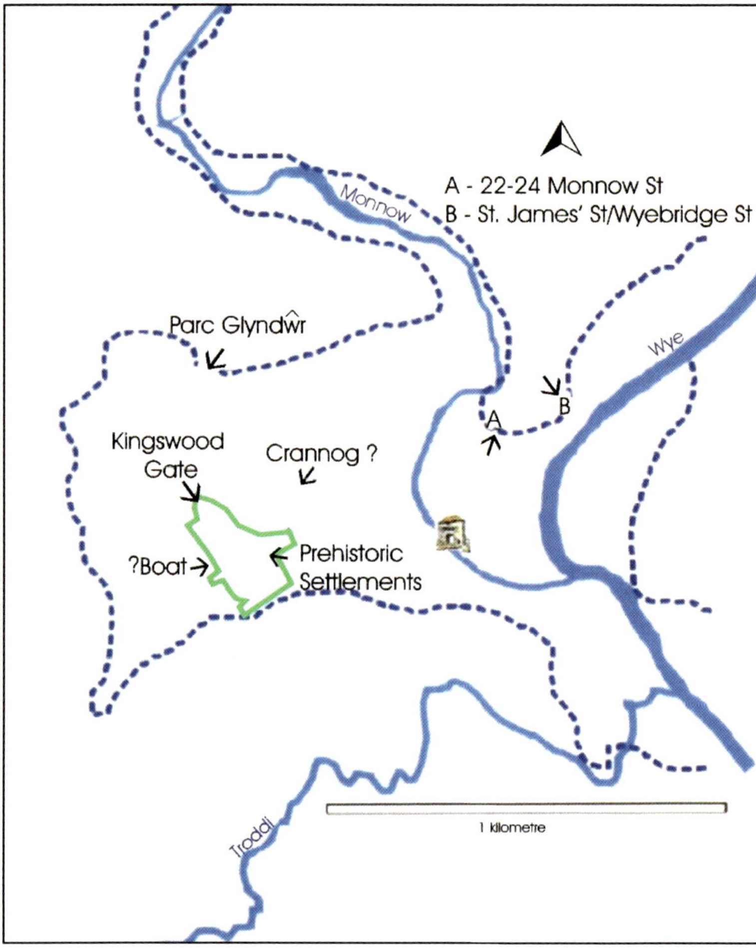

A late phase of the Monmouth post-glacial lake with some of the sites of Stone Age and later activities. *Jane Bray*

The dotted line is the approximate shore of the lake which seems to have been further reduced by the later Iron Age.

The documentary and archaeological evidence is that the town was tidal during some of the Middle Ages.

The Boar Hunt to Llyn Lliwan and the Millstones in the Monmouth Lake

LLYN LLIWAN was where it was described as being in the Mabinogion epic of Culhwch and Olwen – that is at the junction of the Monnow and Wye Valleys. The obvious route from the Vale of Ewyas to the mouth of the Wye (Aber Gwy) was down the Monnow Valley and then down the Wye Valley. This journey would have taken them to the lake of Llyn Lliwan and it was on the shore of the lake that a most interesting incident is described. This one event, in the lake, shows conclusively that Llyn Lliwan was indeed based on a memory the Monmouth Lake:

> *'Twrch Trwyth then passed between Tawy and Ewias. Arthur summoned Cornwall and Devon to meet him at Aber Hafren (the Severn Estuary) and Arthur said to the men of this Island, 'Twrch Trwyth has killed many of my men. By the might of men, he will not go to Cornwall while I am alive. I shall pursue him no more but will engage him in mortal combat. You do what you will.'*

The hunt had caught up with Twrch Trwyth by the lake but in the attempts to grab the treasures (the comb, shears and razor) from between his ears, as required by the trials set by Ysbaddaden, two of the knights ended up in the water.

They had reached the lake on that route before the mouth of the Wye which suggests that the lake was in the Lower Wye Valley or even in the Monnow Valley – we believe that it was at the junction of the two – the Monmouth Lake.

> *This is what happened on his advice: they sent an army of horsemen, and the hounds of the Island with them, as far as Ewias, and they returned from there to the Hafren, and ambushed him with every experienced soldier in this Island, and drove him by sheer force into the Hafren. And Mabon son*

of Modron went with him on Gwyn Myngddwn, Gweddw's steed, into the Hafren, and Gorau son of Custennin and Menw son of Teirgwaedd, between Llyn Lliwan and Aber Gwy.

This time the fight at first went more in the hunters' favour and Twrch Trwyth was forced into the water (referred to as the 'Hafren' – the tidal Severn – the water joining the lake which was backed up by the tide in the narrow gorge below Monmouth). It appears that it is being suggested that they were in the lake itself.

And Arthur fell upon Twrch Trwyth, together with the warriors of Prydain. Osla Gyllellfawr approached, and Manawydan son of Life and Cacamwri, Arthur's servant, and Gwyngelli,and closed in on him. And they grabbed him first by his feet, and soused him in the Hafren until it flooded over him. Mabon son of Modron spurred his horse on the one side and grabbed the razor from him, and on the other side Cyledyr Wyllt rushed into the Hafren on another horse and snatched the shears from him. Before they could remove the comb he found his feet, and firm ground, and from the moment he found dry land neither hound nor man nor steed could keep up with him until he reached Cornwall. Whatever trouble was had getting those treasures from him, worse was had trying to save the two men from drowning. As Cacamwri was pulled up, two millstones pulled him back into the depths. As he was running after the boar Osla Gyllellfawr's knife fell from its sheath and he lost it, and after that his sheath was full of water: as he was pulled up, it pulled him back into the depths.

Penallt millstones on the banks of the Wye just below Monmouth where the knight Cacamwri was being rescued during the boar hunt but 'two millstones kept pulling him down into the depths'. Pwll Mawr Wood and Washings Wood are on the right of the picture.
Photograph: Peter Bere

This extraordinary incident is momentous and is the only mention of millstones in the story; it convincingly confirms that the struggle was meant to have taken place in the Wye Valley just below Monmouth and the lost lake where millstones were cut from the local conglomerate until the 19th century and where examples are still to be found in the woods and along the riverbank.

Millstones from the Penallt quarries which overlooked the Wye and the Monmouth Lake were well known and were even exported down the river to the Continent. We have found examples during excavations on local water mills, some dated to the time of the Culhwch ac Olwen story and some earlier.

So there appears to be no better candidate in Wales, or, for that matter, considering the millstones, anywhere this side of the quarries of Derbyshire!

Happily, Cacamwri must have survived the ordeal for he reappears in the story later. The event, which was imagined to have taken place on hard ground beside the millstone quarries, also suggests that the storyteller considered that the tide this far up the Wye Valley was still part of the Severn (tidal Hafrenwater).

But although the razor and shears were snatched from him, Twrch Trwyth managed to escape and *'before they could get the comb he found his feet and firm ground and from the moment he found dry land neither hound nor man nor steed could keep up with him'*.

This is hardly evocative of a 'tidal' lake in the wide waters and mudflats of the Severn estuary, but does sound very much like the valley of the Wye between Monmouth and Chepstow. Here, the river flowed through a forbidding valley shrouded by steep cliffs and dark forests and where there was no road until the 19th century.

Honor Clarke on millstones abandoned in the woods above the Wye

There are some interesting place names in and around the Monmouth Lake; as well as the Livox Wood on the southern edge of the lake already mentioned. On the Welsh side of the river, above the Colman Rocks is 'Pwll Mawr Wood': the Wood of the 'Great Lake, Pond or Pit' which may refer to the lake or to the tidal water where Cacamwri was nearly drowned by the two millstones or again it might be associated with the millstone quarries in the woods here.

Also this must be where Arthur and his men *'fell upon Twrch Trwyth and grabbing him first by the feet they soused him in the Hafren until it flooded over him'*. Could this possibly be commemorated by the strangely named 'Washing's Wood' and Washing's Lane on the (tidal) riverbank? – more research required.

Other authors have tried to equate the name of Troggy (or the Nedern) with Twrch Trwyth (in this Evans *et al* cite, but dismiss, Codrington 1903 and Barber and Pykitt 1903). Then, of course, there's the Troddi, one of the trio of rivers which fed the lake and today join the River Wye at the head of the lower Wye gorge.

Broken Roman millstone from King's Wood Gate, 2nd or 3rd century

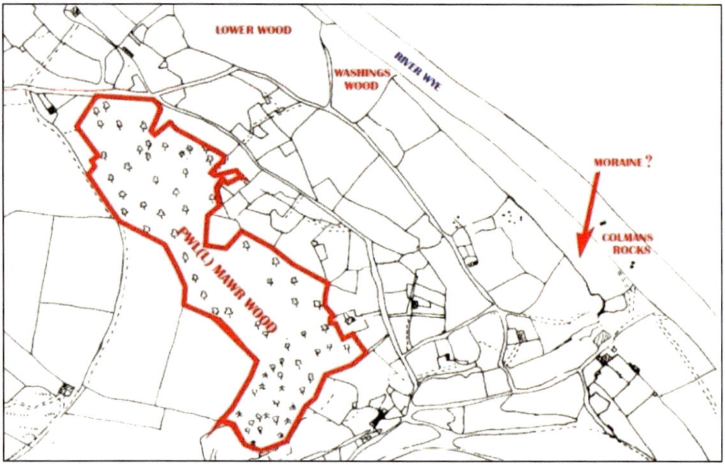

Pwl (Pwll) Mawr Wood ('The Great Lake, Pond or Pit') on the Welsh bank of the Wye below Monmouth and the site of a watery struggle with Twrch Trwyth. Also on the riverside here are the strangely named Washings Wood and Washings Lane. Jane Bray

The Colman Rocks in the River Wye, looking down to Redbrook

Winter mists create an illusion of Llyn Lliwan – from Lydart

The hunting of Twrch Trwyth – the site of the bank of Llyn Lliwan.

Could this jug spout represent the mythical Boar, Twrch Trwyth?

It was the work of a Monmouth potter in around AD1240

Raised lettering on a pot from a similar context to the boar jug

Folk Memories

PERHAPS the ultimate test for a folk memory is where something such as a place or a building, which no-one knew existed, is discovered archaeologically and can then be linked to a legend or folk-tale known (and of course preferably published) prior to the discovery. The tale of Llyn Lliwan appears to be a good example.

A folk memory of the lake may have been reinforced by its having once existed beside a major east-west trading and invasion route from southern England across Wales. The recall of the lake might also have been extended for long after it was drained as the archaeology shows that the site was marked by a huge area of swamp and marshland which has left thick deposits of peat and anaerobic clay around the western flood plains of Monmouth.

In Monmouth there are some interesting place names associated with Roman forts and a Roman villa which were only discovered during the late 20th century. The name Castlefield Farm, for the site of the First-Century Roman fort we found at Kentchurch in the Monnow Valley and the name Berry Farm (Bury?) in woodland beside the Roman forts at Court Farm, Wonastow, which overlooks Monmouth from the west, are good examples.

Another is our discovery, in the 1960s, of a Roman villa in a remote field on the edge of the Dean Forest at Hadnock. This villa, now pretty well destroyed by ploughing, was no lowly hovel as there were hypocaust flue tiles, tegula and tesserae amongst the ruins of the building. This part of the field was also the site of a ghost story, 'The Faceless Lady of Hadnock,' which I had published a decade earlier in the *Monmouthshire Beacon* (and has been re-published by others several times since). Strange indeed, is the site as marked on the tithe map for this part of what was a larger field had the very peculiar name of 'Greens House'.

However, in these cases it seems likely that the names may have been bestowed following the uncovering of structural remains or other relics during ploughing.

Some farmers (perhaps most working on the flood plain) knew of the existence of an ancient lake around Monmouth from their observations during ploughing. Lindsay Ward, whose family has worked the fields around Croft-y-Bwla and the Bailey Pit for generations, always knew the shoreline of the lake from the change in the pebbly soils around the edge of the flood plain. Of course he had no idea of when the lake existed but was not at all surprised when we announced our prehistoric discoveries. In *The Lost Lake* I recorded Dave Pritchard's observation during field-walking the plough of the flood plain in Troy Meadow that all the worked flints appeared to be above a certain level and I recall that we had found mainly microliths for harpoons in the surface of the natural under the shops of Monnow Street – presumably the bed of the ancient lake.

When I was first digging in Trellech, perhaps forty years ago, I was told by an elderly resident that the town had not originally been in Trellech Village but had been along the Catbrook Road. At the time I thought that it was a similar piece of folklore to that associated with the Trellech Tump which was said to have been the burial mound of Saxons killed in a great battle with the Welsh. Later, another farmer said that he had once seen houses as parch-marks alongside the Catbrook Road from a hillside – I think it was from Trellech Beacon; of course, we now know that they were right.

Then there is the Monmouth post-glacial Lake which has only been identified in recent years but which seems to have survived, at least in part, into the Middle Ages and gave rise to features in the Welsh folk tales recorded in the Mabinogion as well as descriptions by the medieval monks, Nennius and Geoffrey of Monmouth. This lake was formed at the close of the last Ice Age and attracted settlement around its shores and even in its waters during all prehistoric times from the Middle Stone Age to the coming of the Romans. It may even have been seriously reduced by the Romans themselves to create pastureland from a rich swampy bog-land which even today has never been totally drained.

The whereabouts of the fabled lake has been a source of speculation for folklorists and an inspiration for authors and mystics ever since the Mabinogion tales were first translated from the Welsh in the 19th century.

In suggesting a home for the legendary lake, past researchers have been misled by the apparent absence of a lake in south-east Wales – a lake which could have been the inspiration for the story of Llyn Lliwan. Consequently, not aware of the Monmouth Lake, it was suggested that Llyn Lliwan was a tidal lake in the River Severn. Although other theories were put forward and while a tidal lake, whatever that was meant to be, did not fit the story or the wide estuary and the muddy foreshores of the Severn, the idea took hold and became the established theory. For instance, in the most recent translation of the Mabinogion, Sioned Davies, former Chair of Welsh at Cardiff University, simply says: '*Llyn Lliw: probably the same place as Llyn Lliwan, mentioned on p.212, a tidal lake somewhere on the Severn estuary*'. It is frustrating to record, but academics we have contacted have not been interested in reconsidering their views.

To fit the Mabinogion story and keep the lake above the mouth of the Wye (it was reached first during the boar hunt) various authors have diverted the hunt through, or even around, the Forest of Dean. However, if they had simply followed the hunt as described in the story they would have come to the lake, for Llyn Lliwan is precisely where it was described as being in the Mabinogion epic of Culhwch and Olwen as being between the Vale of Ewyas and the mouth of the River Wye at Chepstow – at Monmouth.

Some of the early settlements attracted by the lake include two 6,000 to 8,000-year-old hunter-gatherers' camp sites of the Middle Stone Age overlooking the lake from where is now St James' Street and Wyebridge Street. They were followed by people of the New Stone Age who were using buildings which were sometimes set on flat-bottomed stilts (to stop them sinking into the mud) beside and apparently in the lake, some 4,000 to 5,000 years ago. These were the Stone Age settlers who left what appear to be parts of a Stone Age logboat on the lakeside.

Penallt medieval church, overlooking the outflow of the lake near the millstone quarries. The church is said to be sliding down the hill

The Monmouth Lake – Llyn Lliwan

UNTIL the recognition of the site of the ancient lake in Monmouth no lake was known in the region of the Mabinogion epic so the idea arose that Llyn Lliwan was a tidal lake in the Severn. But the Severn is not a lake and the medieval records of both Geoffrey of Monmouth and of Nennius can be seen as casting serious doubt on the interpretation – or, rather, eliminating it.

It was not that long after the retreat of the ice sheets that Middle Stone Age hunter-gatherers were setting up their camps overlooking the lake and these were followed by settlements and activities throughout prehistory.

Archaeological research shows that the lake survived for thousands of years and that there were settlements in and around its shores from the Mesolithic into historical times. As the lake was recorded during the Middle Ages it should have been known to the Romans who, we have suggested, may have been responsible for attempts to drain it.

All lakes and ponds silt up to go through swamp, bog and marshland phases to become dry ground, so the site of the lake could have been recognisable for a long time after it was reduced in size – probably even into the later Middle Ages when it was situated beside, or marked by, a great marsh and a forest of wetland plants. Even today, local people talk of the wetlands between Wonastow Road and The Bailey Pit as a ridiculous place on which to build housing estates. Such a background could have contributed to the 'folk memory' of Llyn Lliwan, while the three rivers in flood may also have occasionally re-created the lake.

The discovery of the Monmouth Lake has been followed by the realisation that it fits the description and location of the mythical Llyn Lliwan and that it may have been the inspiration for an important part of the hunting of Twrch Trwyth in the Culhwch and Olwen story.

Culhwch and the Boar Hunt

The Story of Culhwch ac Olwen in the Mabinogion

ANLAWDD Wledig, the wife of Cilydd Wledig, was pregnant with a son who would be called Culhwch but she went mad and kept away from society until her time was due when she regained her senses and gave birth in a pig-sty and the swineherd raised the boy until he came to court. The baby was baptised Culhwch as he had been born in a pig-run but he was of aristocratic descent for he was a cousin of King Arthur although raised by foster-parents.

At court, his step-mother wanted him to marry her own daughter but Culhwch said that he was too young; at this his mother shouted 'I swear a destiny on you that your side shall never strike against a woman until you get Olwen daughter of Ysbaddaden Bencawr.' At the mention of Olwen's name and without even setting eyes on her, Culhwch falls madly in love with her.

But if Olwen was to marry Culhwch it would mean the death of her father, Ysbaddaden, who was to set a series of near-impossible tasks before he would agree to the marriage. Now very upset, the boy went to his father who said that he was not to worry as it would be easy. 'Go to your cousin, King Arthur and have your hair trimmed and ask him for help as your gift.'

And so . . . off went Culhwch on a grey-headed steed four winters old with well-jointed stride, shell-like hooves and a gold bridle-bit in its mouth and a gold saddle beneath him, with two silver spears in his hand. He had a battle-axe in his right hand which could draw blood from the wind and he wore a gold-hilted sword with a gold chased shield with a rim of ivory. One of the hardest trials was to win several treasures from between the ears of the formidable boar, Twrch Trwyth, who had been transformed by magic from an evil king of Ireland.

After the crossing of the Irish Sea to Pembrokeshire, the hunting of Twrch Trwyth took the heroes from West Wales to northern Gwent where they reached the Vale of Ewyas and the River Honddu which joins the Monnow at Llanfihangel Crucornau. From there the Monnow runs east, past Grosmont and Skenfrith, to join the Wye at Monmouth. Obviously the route to Aber Gwy at Chepstow from here would have been down the Monnow and Wye Valleys and it was at the junction of the Monnow and Wye that the hunt came upon the lost lake called Llyn Lliwan.

The footprint of a medieval boar – preserved on a roof tile from the 15th century floor tile kiln at Cadogan House, Monmouth

The King Arthur story and Twrch Trwyth

IN AN inventively anachronistic way, the tale of Culhwch and Olwen superimposes King Arthur and his Court in a story which includes what may have been a folk memory of the long vanished Monmouth Lake. Culhwch goes to the Court of his cousin King Arthur at Tintagel (or Caerleon?) to ask for aid and Arthur calls up some two hundred of his greatest knights, with women, dogs, horses and swords, to support the chase. First they have to find Mabon, the hunter, son of Modron, who was taken from his mother when just three nights old.

Along with Gwrhyr Gwalstawd Iethoedd, who could speak all human languages as well as some of those of the birds and beasts and with help from a number of increasingly ancient animals – the Blackbird of Cilgwri, the Stag of Rhedynfre; the Owl of Cwm Cawlwyd and the Eagle of Gwernabwy, they are led across country to Llyn Lliwan.

In the lake, the Salmon of Llyn Lliw was said to have been the oldest animal in the world and he aided the quest to rescue Mabon the hunter, asking that Arthur's men first take fifty fish spears out of his back. Two men rode the salmon to Gloucester (the Severn bore?) to the rescue of Mabon. It is worth remembering that the River Wye abounded in fish, especially salmon, as one of the most famous salmon fishing rivers in Europe where indentures record that masters should not feed their apprentices on salmon more than so many times in a week – it was so cheap and plentiful that they were likely to give them nothing else.

The hunt, now underway from Pembrokeshire, crossed southern Wales to reach, after many deaths and adventures, the Vale of Ewyas, north of Grosmont. The Twrch then swerved south, down the Monnow Valley towards the mouth of the Wye (Aber Gwy) with the hounds is close pursuit. Coming down from the north, the route would have followed the Monnow Valley to arrive where the two rivers meet the River Troddi – at the Monmouth Lake – which we suggest was the original Llyn Lliwan.

The enduring interest for Celtic Studies has been to ask if there was ever a real Llyn Lliwan and where it had been. The cause of the problem has been that there was no known lake in south-east Wales. Of course that has now changed with the recent discovery that there really had been a freshwater lake in the region described in the story and one which fits the description as one of Nennius's 'Wonders of the World': *Linn Lliwan*. The identification of the Monmouth Lake as the mythical lake has been confirmed by archaeological discoveries in and around the site of the lake at Monmouth.

By following the obvious and practical route of the mythical boar hunt across southern Wales to Ewyas and then down the Monnow Valley to Monmouth – straight to the enchanted lake.

The rescue of Modron from Gloucester in the early part of the story only shows that a salmon could swim from the lake down to the Severn and on to Gloucester while the subsequent tale of the adventure after reaching the lake and catching up with the boar is far more informative and vital to establishing the whereabouts of the original inspiration for the legend of Llyn Lliwan.

And we should never forget the parts played by magic lakes in Welsh folklore and especially in the legends of King Arthur and *Excalibur*.

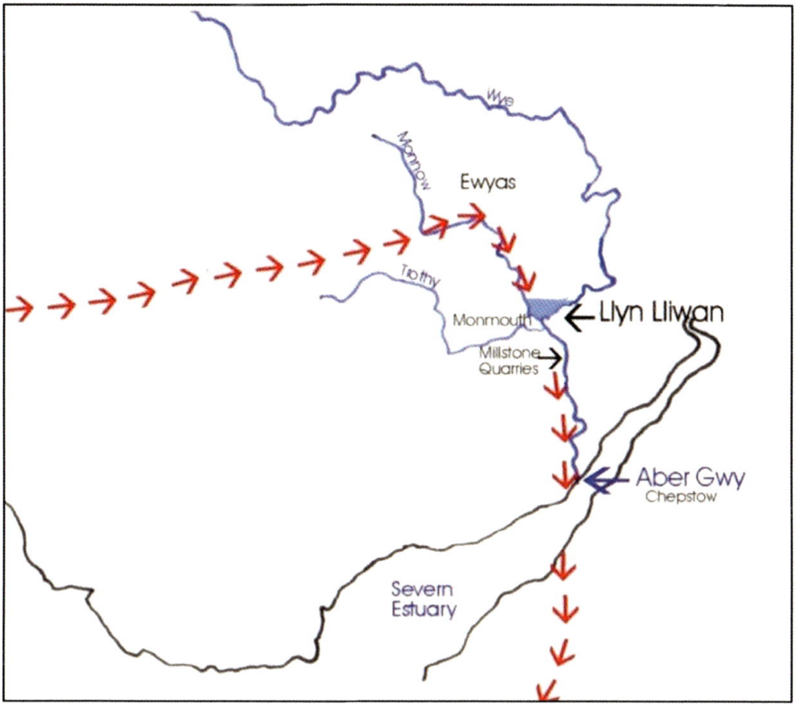

Jane Bray

The obvious route of the hunting of Twrch Trwyth from the Vale of Ewyas to the mouth of the Wye (Aber Gwy) at Chepstow – down the Monnow Valley and the Wye Valley via Llyn Lliwan.
Here the hunt would pass beside the Penallt millstone quarries.

It is important to note that the suggested deviations of the hunt to the east by other authors were intended to put the lake above the mouth of the Wye as it was reached first in the story, but we should remember that the heroes were not by then coming from west to east but from north to south, down from the Vale of Ewyas.

Also, taking the hunt into England through the Forest of Dean, to put Llyn Lliwan above the mouth of the Wye, is very circuitous compared with the direct and obvious route from the banks of the Honddu to the River Monnow and down to Aber Gwy at Chepstow to reach an implausible 'tidal lake' in the Severn Estuary. Now we know that they would have passed by the real lake at Monmouth.

Another ploy to keep the new make-believe lake tidal and in the Severn was to remove Ewyas from the story altogether and keep the hunt going west to east – not north to south – again putting the tidal lake in the Severn and above Aber Gwy.

But now, back to the lake and the knights of King Arthur where, after catching up with the boar and a fight on the banks of the lake at Monmouth two of his men are left drowning in the water.

The case for the Monmouth Lake being Llyn Lliwan in the story of Culhwch ac Olwen is threefold; firstly, it is precisely where it is described as being during the great Arthurian boar hunt (between Ewyas and Aber Gwy); secondly, The lake and its preserved historical alluvial features are just what was recorded as taking place by Nennius and Geoffrey of Monmouth during the 9th and 12th centuries and thirdly, the incident with the millstones in the hunting of Twrch Trwyth can only have been envisaged as taking place beside the millstone quarries of Penallt and therefore in the Monmouth Lake itself. *[for maps of the hunt across Wales, see page 82 and 83]*

Machine scrape in lake bed below peat/pondweed marl - Siltbusters

A Prehistoric Lake Village

The Siltbusters attenuation pond covers extensive prehistoric settlements with radiocarbon dates extending over millennia.

Siltbusters attenuation pond: On part of the site of Llyn Lliwan where there are fifteen hundred years of prehistoric settlements – often on stilts – preserved under the water of the modern attenuation pond.

There is a collapsed but well-preserved Bronze Age timber structure and burnt mound, with pottery, some bone and brushwood floors with scores of unopened hazel nuts (in the distance on the right).

The remains produced a radiocarbon date of 4458BP while the 'stilts' of other buildings were very much older.

These four flat-bottomed posts are from the bed of the lake. They have Bronze Age and New Stone Age dates. The ivy-twisted pole on the left is from the floor of the Bronze Age hut.

The later Stone Age settlement of Llyn Lliwan, a reconstruction by Peter Bere. (From 'The Lost Lake')

A Neolithic Structure set in the lake

AT Jordan Way, some 800 metres to the east of the King's Wood Gate development, the base of a large oak post, with a carefully tooled flat base (with a stone axe), presumably to prevent sinkage, had been set upright in the lake bed and may have been part of a Neolithic structure on stilts. This structure could be related to the possible boat timbers (pages 85-87) as they have radiocarbon dates of 4867 years BP against 5160 years BP.

Further evidence from around this time came from the footprint of the Siltbuster new main building where a hearth containing worked Neolithic style flints produced a radiocarbon date of 4882 years BP.

The post at Jordan Way was preserved in 2003 by Martin Tuck of the Glamorgan-Gwent Archaeological Trust during a watching brief on the new houses then being built off Watery Lane. The clay and peat deposits were similar to those at Parc Glyndŵr and those on the other Wonastow Road developments. Jordan Way would have been out from the shore of the lake so could have been under water until at least the end of the Iron Age. The radiocarbon date was 4867 years BP.

Neolithic (the New Stone Age) – almost 5,000 years old. As the structure would have been out from the shore of the lake and in fairly deep water it seems to be part of something like a crannog structure.

If the post was part of a crannog it appears to be a lot older than any of the dated Irish ones which appear from 1200-600 BC and it is well up there with the Scottish crannogs which range from 3650 to 2500 BC. It is some 4,000 years older than the only known crannog in Wales – that at Llangors, near Brecon – which is late 10th century and thought to have been the royal residence of the King of Brycheiniog. More recently there have been the remarkable late Bronze Age discoveries with unsurpassed preservation at Must Farm in Cambridgeshire. We are grateful to the Glamorgan-Gwent Archaeological Trust and Martin Tuck for help and for permission to obtain the radiocarbon date from the Jordan Way timber.

The piece retains much of its bark and is around 130mm long and 125mm across. The end was trimmed flat with lots of the cutting facets facing outward and not from the bark inward. The cuts, which would have been made with a stone or flint axe, appear to show that the cutting edge of the tool was some 40mm wide and that the average depth of cut was just 0.5cm. The setting of the levelled end of the post in the bed of the lake caused its preservation under the anaerobic conditions. It was set upright in the lake bed, like a stilt, the flat end at the bottom helping to prevent sinkage.

It is hard to imagine what this large timber was for if it was not a 'stilt' for a structure set on the lake bed. We imagine that it was a support for a level platform or a floor, perhaps with the flat base of the post resting upon a wood or stone post pad like those found in the foundations of other wetland structures and best illustrated by those at Hornstaad-Hörnle in Germany by John and Bryony Coles' *'Enlarging the Past'* (1995, p35).

This New Stone Age polished flint axe was found by Simon Gleed less than 500 metres from the shore of the lake at Parc Glyndŵr (SO 48611 13447).
It would have been the type of tool used to work the timbers for the prehistoric structures. Reprinted from 'The Lost Lake'.
Mr Gleed has kindly donated the axe to Monmouth Museum.

Crannogs are widespread in Ireland with an estimated 1,200 examples while in Scotland there are 347 of them. Crannogs are sometimes depicted as farmhouses, often as defensive settlements or, as in the case of Llangors, as royal sites of power and status. The Llangors crannog is fairly close to the shore while the Monmouth site may have been further out into the lake.

Watching briefs during the excavation of the two flood attenuation ponds at Overmonnow (Barratt Homes and Siltbusters) have revealed prehistoric settlements, including a Bronze Age collapsed wooden structure – possibly a wooden round house – with potsherds, environmental remains and a burnt mound (radiocarbon date of 2458 years BP).

The wooden stilt-like foundations on the Siltbusters attenuation pond site seem to spread from the Bronze Age domestic site out into the lake with radiocarbon dates of 2582 BP, 2505BP and 4223 years BP. Bones are not common on the bed of the lake but they have occasionally survived, such as one on Plot 191 which has produced a radiocarbon date of 3006 ±24 BP.

Peter Bere's reconstruction of a Monmouth crannog.

Other Settlements in and beside the lake

EXCAVATIONS for a flood attenuation pond for Siltbusters on what seems to have been marsh or swamp land in or beside the lake during the Bronze Age, exposed the remains of timber structures associated with a burnt mound of pot boiler stones.

After the building had been abandoned the site appears to have been flooded, leaving small areas of very fine sand over some of the remains. The surviving timbers were sealed by peat under a layer of anaerobic 'estuarine' clay which was then followed by topsoil phases. Scores of unopened hazel nuts were scattered over a wide area amongst the brushwood which had been brought in to cover the earthen floors; presumably the nuts came in on the brushwood. They were radiocarbon dated to 2458 years BP and 2483 years BP. Amongst the timbers and brushwood there were areas of light-coloured clay which may be de-natured daub.

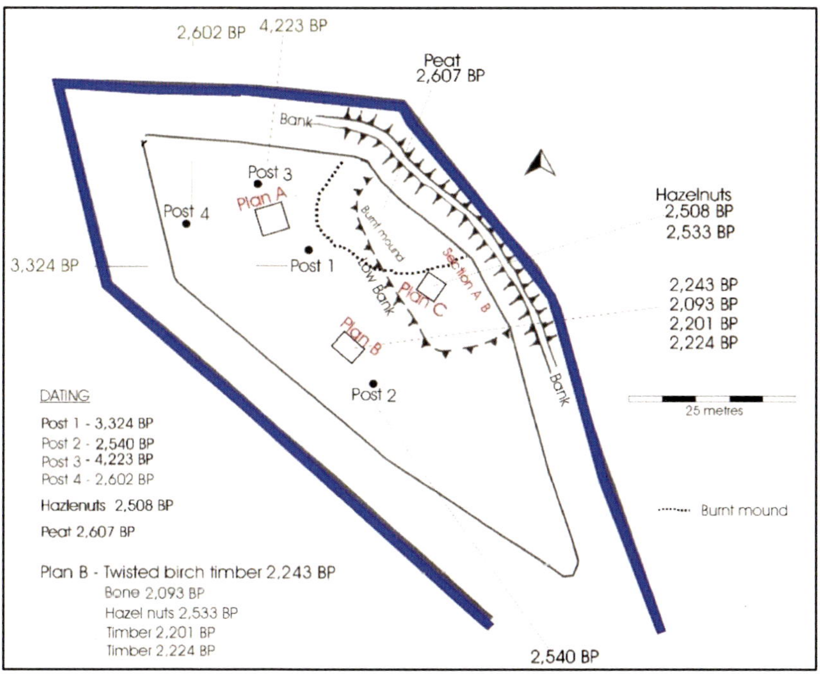

A series of posts set in the lake bed in the Siltbusters attenuation pond were dated between 2490 years and 4173 years BP (see plan page 63) as they were associated with scattered timbers indicating a very long period of settlement, apparently in and beside the lake itself; the posts were shallowly set in the lake bed and, like the single post from Jordan Way, were flat-bottomed, presumably to prevent sinkage. The remains, where possible, were preserved in-situ.

The burnt mound and the collapsed structure which was associated with Bronze Age pottery, some bone and scores of unopened hazel nuts, appears to support the idea that this area was either dry ground or marsh. However, it must have been near enough to the lake to be flooded by slowly moving water in order to carry fine sand in suspension; the hazel nuts were presumably brought in with the brushwood on the floors, suggesting that it was gathered during late summer.

A post in Plot 275 produced a date of 5930 years ± 30 BP.

The remains of prehistoric settlements, some on stilts, are preserved beneath the water of the Siltbusters attenuation pond

Bronze Age potsherds from the Siltbusters burnt mound

Bronze Age bone and hazel nuts from the Siltbusters hut floor

The attenuation pond with the Bronze Age domestic building was flooded during one stormy day and night and the site was left under water for the rest of the season in order to keep the remains preserved before a planned part excavation, recording and preservation in situ, could take place during the following year.

However, when the time came in 2017 to begin the work it was found that newts and frogs and other wildlife had moved in and made their homes in the pond. Consequently, as the developers' depth for the attenuation pond had reached its planned depth, there was no threat to the archaeology, it was agreed that the wildlife could best be conserved if the archaeological remains were preserved in situ.

With the developers' cooperation, it was decided that amphibians would be excellent protection for the archaeology – against both developers and archaeologists – so they continue as the guardians of the undisturbed remains.

The brushwood and timber inside a collapsed wooden building in the Siltbusters flood pond. With white clay daub, fine flood silts, Bronze Age pottery and hazel nuts. Radiocarbon dating from 2458 to 4173 years BP. The remains were not disturbed below this surface.

Post 11.5 cm WIDE

Post 1 in the Siltbusters flood pond. This flat-bottomed post was set in the bed of the lake and produced a date of 3274 years BP

Post 2. This post was set vertically but shallowly in the bed of the lake (and later bent over). It produced a date of 2490 years BP

A Bronze Age pole on a hut floor, presumably twisted by Ivy.

Peter Bere's reconstruction of the Bronze Age settlement

Barratt's attenuation ponds where the prehistoric settlements and a possible later Roman vineyard are preserved under the water.

The Siltbuster attenuation pond – the first phase of the preservation of the prehistoric remains.

The Siltbusters attenuation pond. The areas containing timber at the surface, near the domestic settlement in the compound in the middle of the top photograph was covered with Teram and then preserved in situ. Some timber and brushwood over the burnt mound was carefully cleared of wildlife and covered with Teram and now remains undisturbed. As planned by the developers, a thin layer of loam was spread over the bed of the pond to facilitate the growth of marsh and aquatic vegetation, and to encourage wildlife.

A provisional timeline for The Lake

Before 11,000 years ago:	Ice Age creation of the Monmouth bowl by glaciers and trapped ice.
Until 11,000 years ago:	Ice Lake and glaciers.
After 11,000 years ago:	Fresh-water lake of melt-water.
Before 6,000 years ago:	Deep water lake over most of Monmouth bowl – Mesolithic shore probably to Agincourt Square?
Before 2,500 years ago:	Mesolithic shore below Agincourt Square to St James' Street storm deposit? of pebbles and sand.
After 2,500 years ago:	Early Bronze Age shore at 20 Monnow Street.
	Early BA to Late IA – No change.
By 1st century	The Lake is still in place but apparently much lower.
Before cAD100	Later Iron Age occupation overlooking lake from St James' St.
	Pond marl forming at Parc Glyndŵr
1st century or earlier	Large lake drained, start? of peat.
	Lake to Marsh; filling with peat.
By 1st century AD	Roman Fort on the edge of lake at 20 Monnow Street.
	Roman pottery and slag in the bed of the lake – Town Wall, 30 MS etc.
By the 2nd century	Roman occupation on lake bed.
	Roman coin in peat in flood pond.
	King's Wood Roman iron-working.
19th and 20th centuries	Extensive attempts at field drainage
	New estates built on the flood plain.
Anomaly	Microlith in peat.

Kingswood drainage on higher ground – no peat but alluvial clay

'Pondweed marl below the peat – Siltbusters attenuation pond

A Bronze Age burnt mound (black) covered with peat below the 'estuarine' clay, in the Siltbusters' attenuation pond. Looking south.

Channels cutting a burnt mound at Parc Glyndŵr with alluvial clay.

Peat (with Roman coin) filling a channel at King's Wood Gate

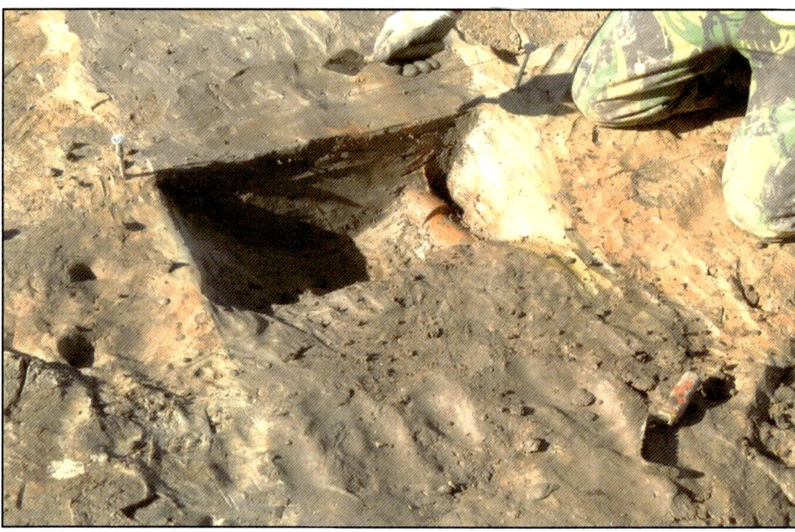

Peat filling a channel cut into alluvial clay. The pipe was 'mole' driven, not cut in from above.

Both Nennius and Geoffrey of Monmouth describe Llyn Lliwan as being a lake on a river which runs into the Severn and was filled (or topped up) by the tide. They both describe the same 'outburst' at the ebbing of the tide. Their reference to the 'Teared'– 'tear'or 'break'? may refer to the Wye dividing into the three rivers at the Monmouth lake.

It seems that the alluvial clay must have arrived with the inflow of the tide and slack water and was left behind after the tidal outburst of water receded.

The clay breaks down into muddy water and re-creates itself as clay when it dries along the shores of the lake and in the hollows and archaeological features.

Sea levels appear to have have dropped after Geoffrey's time so that the tides may not have reached the site of the lake and its shore or the surrounding flood plain. Also today, Gordon McDonald pointed out, there are new bridges and weirs which slow the tide.

St James' House, rear garden, over the bed of the lake at 1.30m to 1.60m; Roman pottery and a re-touched flint. 4.4.16

St James' House, rear garden; just above the bed of the lake at 1.30m to 1.60m; Iron slag, unlike normal bloomery waste, 4/4/16. There were similar but heavier deposits at 2.5m below ground level to the rear of 30 Monnow Street

Barratt's attenuation pond – preserving prehistoric settlements

The rain-washed gravel bed of the post-glacial lake (at Barratt's attenuation pond)

This triangular piece of sandstone came from the bed of the lake at E=349205.917 N=213242.213. Level 23.425. (Parc Glyndŵr)
It was the only stone for many plots around and may have been kept for superstitious reasons as the triangle was said to be the Devil's door, where demons were summoned. Witches also used the triangle to view magic.
The stone is 13cm wide and 13cm deep.

A vision of Llyn Lliwan, across Vauxhall from Geoffrey's Window, Monmouth Priory, recreated by the 2020 floods across Vauxhall.

The vision of Llyn Lliwan fades – from below Geoffrey's Window, with the lake and floods drained, 2020.

Geoffrey of Monmouth in a St Mary's Priory Church window

The inspiration for the story of Llyn Lliwan

WE suggest that the inspiration for the Llyn Lliwan story might have been a folk memory of the real lake at Monmouth – at least part of which would have been known in medieval times. The tale of a magical lake of this name in south-east Wales has a long history.

However, the details of the location and some important features of the lake come from the Mabinogion tale of Culhwch ac Olwen and the hunting of the great boar Twrch Trwyth, which was really a transmogrified evil Irish King.

There are some four or five centuries between the Romans (if they had partially drained the lake) and Nennius with a similar period between Nennius and the Mabinogion for the memory of the lake to be lost; so the question of folk memory survival may be relevant here – just how long can a tradition of the Monmouth Lake have endured? (See 'What happened to the Lake?' on page 109).

Significantly, the descriptions by Nennius and Geoffrey of Monmouth of a lake joined to a river or rivers heading for the Severn and closely linked to the tides perfectly fits the Monmouth Lake – the existence and history of which is proven by millennia of archaeological remains and also by the tide being still traceable in Monmouth's River Wye today in and beside the site of the lake.

So we are suggesting that the Mabinogion tale of an ancient lake in the lower Wye Valley may be based on a folk memory of the Monmouth Lake. After all, academics have linked some Welsh myths back to the Iron Age or even earlier (such as the Welsh Fairies – the Tylwyth Teg). In putting the Monmouth Lake forward as a candidate for Llyn Lliwan we must ask how long the real lake had lasted, for if it had drained soon after the Ice Age it could hardly have been established as a folk memory. Now that there is increasing evidence that at least some of the lake survived into the Middle Ages, the possibility of a tradition recalling a huge body of water might have persisted into historical times.

Until now, most of the claims for the site of Llyn Lliwan Lake have either explained it as an 'estuarine' or 'tidal' lake, in the Severn, or one just beside the Severn – an interesting case for an inlet and lake being near Caldicot was put by the enthusiastic researcher, the late John Nettleship, and is still popular amongst some antiquarians.

However, the hunt was coming south from Ewyas in the north to the mouth of the Wye in the south; so Llyn Lliwan has to be upstream of the mouth of the Wye which would rule out Caldicot but, of course, does favour Monmouth.

John Nettleship's anonymous biographer actually leaves out Ewyas altogether and has the hunt continuing west to east and straight to Llyn Lliwan at Caldicot. This of course does mean that the hunt would have reached his lake before the mouth of the Wye – although downstream of it – not from above, as in the story.

So it is important when considering the deviations suggested by folklorists and historians to fit the lake to their versions of the Mabinogion story that we should remember that the heroes were not by then continuing from west to east or up the Severn, or going from south to north, but from north to south – from Ewyas.

Also, taking the hunt through the Forest of Dean to put the lake above the mouth of the Wye appears circuitous and tortuous compared with the direct route down the Monnow Valley (although probably also forested), from Ewyas to Monmouth and on to Chepstow and the Severn.

The hunting of Twrch Trwyth

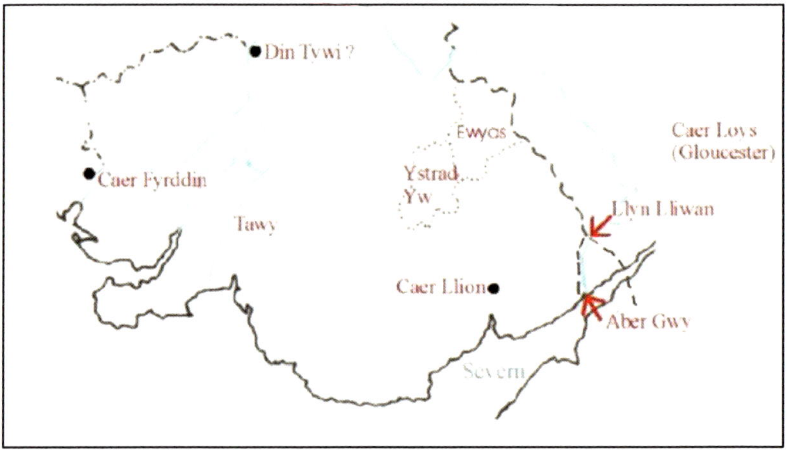

The hunting of Twrch Trwyth – from Ireland and West Wales to Ewyas in northern Gwent, and then down the Welsh border (the Monnow Valley) to Monmouth (with its mythical Lake of Llyn Lliwan).

The route through the Forest of Dean was championed by supporters of a 'tidal lake in the Severn' theory in order to make the hunt reach the River Severn above the mouth of the Wye (Aber Gwy). That was necessary as in the story the chase reached the lake first. The Lake was, according to those researchers, a tidal lake in the Severn Estuary.

However, the route to an imaginary 'tidal lake 'ignores the obvious way down the Monnow and Wye Valleys to the Severn (this would have encountered the real but by now forgotten Lake of Llyn Lliwan in Monmouth). The deviation was of course the only way to make the hunt reach the imagined tidal lake in the Severn – above the mouth of the Wye.

Jane Bray

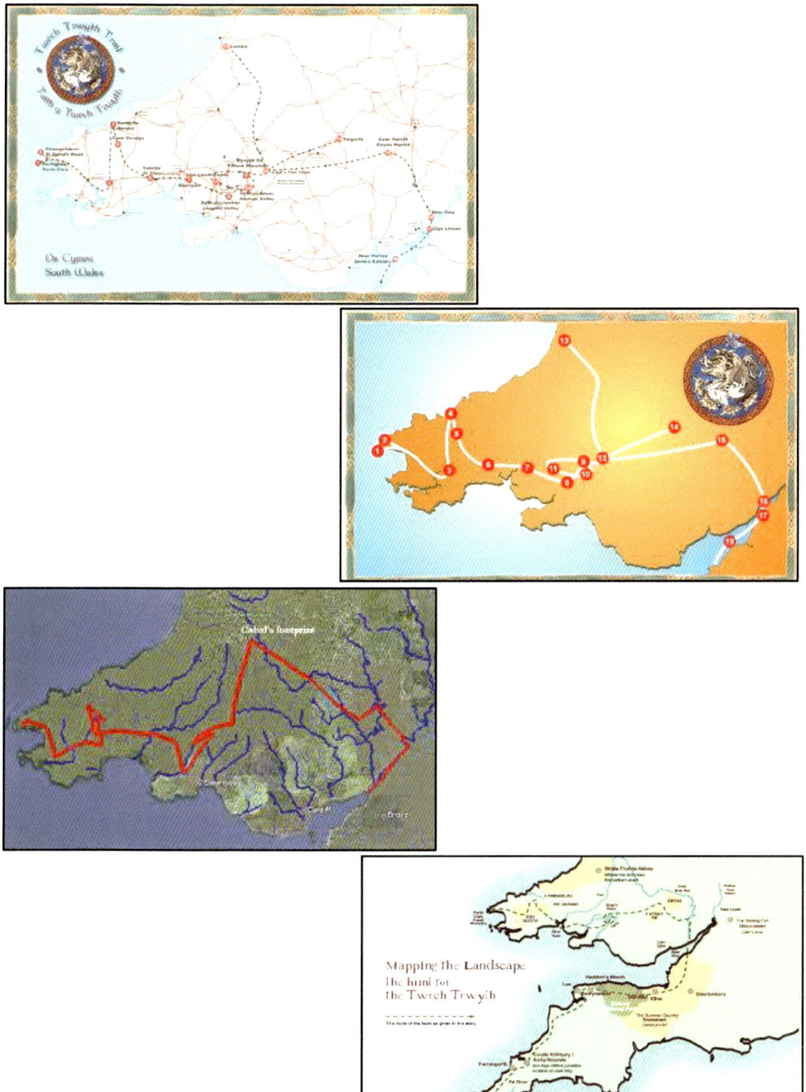

The hunting of Twrch Trwyth: some of the routes from the Vale of Ewyas to Chepstow as suggested by various authors – before the discovery of the Monmouth Lake – They were 'Mabinogion Astronomy'; Damian Bullen; Margaret Jones; Adverse Camber.

Some evidence of the Welsh fascination with Twrch Trwyth

There is even a Welsh folk dance called Dawnswy Twrch Trwyth

A tussle with a Twrch Trwyth piglet in Llyn Lliwan
by Peter Bere

5,000-year-old timbers from the shore of the Lake

FIVE well-preserved New Stone Age timbers, all of oak and all of a similar Neolithic date were recovered from the layer of anaerobic clay which formed over the bed of the lake prior to the end of the life of the lake at King's Wood Gate. Unfortunately, the excavations consisted of the narrow and very deep trenches required for the footings of house foundations which had to extend below the soft peat and clay to the harder gravelly bed of the lake. Although it was too dangerous to enter the trenches on this part of the site, it was clear from the anaerobic clay adhering to the timbers that they had come from immediately beside the presumed edge of the lake. This would have been when the pondweed marl was forming in the fresh water lake and before the growth of the peat began, it would have been where a boat would have rested after being pulled up out of the lake – and subsequently, in this case, burned.

The timbers from King's Wood Gate are centred on a hollowed-out log and one of them was radiocarbon dated by the Scottish Universities Environmental Research Centre to 5160 ± 34 years BP: Sample WON-1-2016 plus or minus 34 years) – during the early to middle of the New Stone Age (the Neolithic). The working of the timbers suggests that they may be parts of a logboat but with very unusual features which may be associated with ropes or even an oar. The problem is that we could find nothing in the literature to match them and subsequent dates show that they were all just over 5,000 years old including the unworked oak log (Sample WOB19-005 (Timber 5): 5024 years BP ± 26 years.

Professor Seán McGrail, Master Mariner and expert on logboats, would not be committed to confirming them as parts of a boat although they meet criteria which he set out for identifying logboats in his *Logboats of England and Wales* in 1978. Here, timbers had to have at least two of six features; the Monmouth timbers appear to meet four of the six (see page 98).

In *'The Lost Lake'* (May, 2016) we suggested that we may have found a prehistoric boat building site and sometimes received a rather frosty reception, some experts being quite hostile. Now we may have found parts of something which appears to match Peter Bere's reconstruction, so we await any reaction to that; it's a pity it's so old!

The dating of the timbers was of course crucial so it was decided to submit samples from the other timbers from the same context and they came out as follows:

Sample WOB18-001 (Timber 1): 5,106 years BP ± 29 years.

Sample WOB18-002 (Timber 2): 5,071 years BP ± 29 years.

Sample WOB 18-003 (Timber 3): 5,070 years BP ± 29 years.

Sample WOB18-004 (Timber 4): 5,082 years BP ± 29 years.

Sample WOB19-005 (Timber 5): 5,024 years BP ± 26 years. This is the unworked oak log.

This suggests that the pieces could all be parts of the same object while the unworked oak log, of a similar date, from the same context, might mean that this was a timber working site of a similar date.

Timber 1. The suggested boat hull with the worn gunwale at the top and the shallow groove on the left. The other worn cut is to the rear of the right hand end of the timber.

Timber 1.
The suggested gunwale from above with the worn oval cut on the right and the wider worn shallow groove on the left.
The wear on the left is at right angles to the 'hull'. The wear on the oval cut suggests that it was caused by a rope running to the right at an upward angle from the left.

Timber 1, with a possible explanation for the cut and worn features.

Timber1. A possible explanation for the cut and worn features.

Background: At this point it may be worth running over the dating of the nearby discoveries for an overall view of the site:
4882 years BP – the Neolithic hearth Siltbusters building site.

4867 years BP – the probable foundation stilt for a Crannog type of structure at Jordan Way (see 'A Neolithic Lake Building')

Other Stone Age wooden structural foundation 'stilts' on the Siltbusters attenuation pond range in date from 4173 years BP to 2570 years BP with another post of 3,980 years BP.

The Bronze Age domestic settlement (with structure, pottery, bone, hazel nuts and burnt mound) was centered on 2458 years BP.

A wooden post on Plot 275 of the Barratt's Homes site was dated at 5930 years BP.

In *'The Lost Lake'* (May, 2016) the article on the 'channels' discovered in 2012 which were cutting one of the Bronze Age burnt mounds put forward the idea that the site was being used for prehistoric boat building. We did not envisage that the Stone Age people were creating simple log boats on the site but more complex vessels – probably something like twin canoes with outriggers and even with sails – boats which could venture far from land to Ireland or the Continent.

The idea came from there being two parallel round-bottomed cuts at Parc Glyndŵr with a third one a little further away with an entirely different and thinner profile. It was imagined that the two round-bottomed channels were where two canoes had been set up while the third cut was for an outrigger. Such a combination boat would have been assembled in the channels before being slid out along the watered clay channels on to the lake. We thought that this would not go down well with other archaeologists, and we were right. There were some encouraging and prestigious reviews of the book (*Journal of Wetland Archaeology; The Antiquaries Journal* and *Archaeologia Cambrensis*). Other reactions were fairly non-committal (and in one case, in *Current Archaeology,* strangely 'hostile') especially towards the reconstruction of a Parc Glyndŵr boat by Peter Bere which showed twin canoes with an outrigger, mast and a sail with ropes.

Although based on Bere's examination and interpretation of the remains at Parc Glyndŵr, there seemed to be nothing like such a vessel in the literature. My explanation was that if such boats had existed they would have been the more likely to have survived journeys across deep water (as some boats must have done) to reach a shore or river bank and end up as firewood or for 'spares' and not preserved at the bottom of rivers, lakes or estuaries.

On the other hand, single logboats which are quite commonly found in such places around Britain and Europe were most unstable and very often ended up preserved in muddy underwater graves.

Even so, under fire, we began to worry about our twin logboats with sails, although there appeared to be evidence that twin logboats had once existed around Britain and Europe – but perhaps not in our complex form. We were especially concerned when we heard about the Hertfordshire discovery of similar channels to the ones cutting the Bronze Age burnt mound at Parc Glyndŵr which were as being explained as cultivation features of a Roman vineyard.

However, some four years later, the recovery of the 5,000-year-old timbers from King's Wood Gate, also on the shore of the lake and not that far away from Parc Glyndŵr, proved to encompass a remarkable coincidence for they looked very much like parts of a boat. The shape of the timbers and the wear on the suspected hull looks remarkably like parts of Peter Bere's interpretation of a Parc Glyndwr twin canoe – and one with a sail too. Also, as 'predicted', most of the pieces had been partially burned. The working of the timbers and the wear on them encourages us to resurrect Bere's Parc Glyndwr vessel – at least until the detractors have also looked again at the evidence. However, the biggest problem – and possibly an insurmountable one is the great age of the timbers as all of them have radiocarbon dates of over 5,000 years before the present.

Also of considerable interest is the unworked log from the same context (Timber 5) which produced a similar date to the worked timbers: 5024 years BP ± 26 years. Others might like to speculate on its significance and implications.

Timber 1, (photos p.93-94) is reminiscent of the gunwale (A-B) towards the stern or the bow of a boat; it has an oval-shaped cut, 4.8cm wide, and cut vertically into the surface of the wider end of the 'gunwale.' If this was to take a rope the wood was broken where the pressure would have been the greatest. There is a shallow U-shaped groove (in the 'stern'?) which, if this is a part of a boat, may have been caused by a steering oar or a punting pole (A). The wear on this cut is at right-angles to the gunwale.

The second worked timber (2) resembles part of the hull of a boat; it has a large round hole, 7.5cm wide, which is cut through it horizontally where there are very strong signs of wear. If part of a boat, the feature may be associated with the attachment of another logboat or an outrigger, a rope, or even an oar.

The wear on the cut Timber 1 appears to be consistent with that caused by a rope running forward but almost vertically up from the cut hole. This should not be the case if a rope was pulling from the cut horizontally as it would have been in some sort of sledge but it would be accurate if it was connecting upwards from the gunwale of a boat to a sail, as in Bere's interpretation.

The other worked features on this and the other main timber only add to the complexity of the imagined vessel. The large 'groove' which was cut further along the presumed gunwale (perhaps towards the rear of the vessel) has a different wear and one which appears as shallow indentations at right angles to the timber. If the 'groove' was made to accommodate a steering oar, one might surmise that the abrasions would tend to be at right angles to the gunwale; however, any wear caused by a punting pole might be different.

The fact is that although twin canoes were apparently in use in Britain and Ireland during prehistoric times nothing precisely like the Peter Bere reconstruction has so far been recognised. Of course, it's the suggestion of a vessel with sails that makes the interpretation so unacceptable to many, although we do know that sea crossings were being made between Britain and Ireland and between Britain and the Continent and that those journeys were very unlikely to have been achieved in single logboats. There is always the seemingly unlikely possibility that, as the Monmouth Lake was accessible from the sea, a more advanced vessel might be from another land.

The Neolithic boat timbers were found during deep drainage excavations on the edge of the lake (or lagoon which seems to have been left when water levels dropped, probably before the Bronze Age). The fifth piece appears to be an unworked oak log (5024 ± 26 BP).

Another interpretation for the larger timber put forward by Gordon McDonald, is that it was part of an upright washstrake.

The timbers were found beside the site of the lake just 1,400 metres south of Parc Glyndŵr where the channels crossing a Bronze Age burnt mound, were published with pottery and radiocarbon dates of: 3765 years BP; 3720 years BP; 3700 years BP; 3630 years BP; 3040 years BP (all ±35)

.

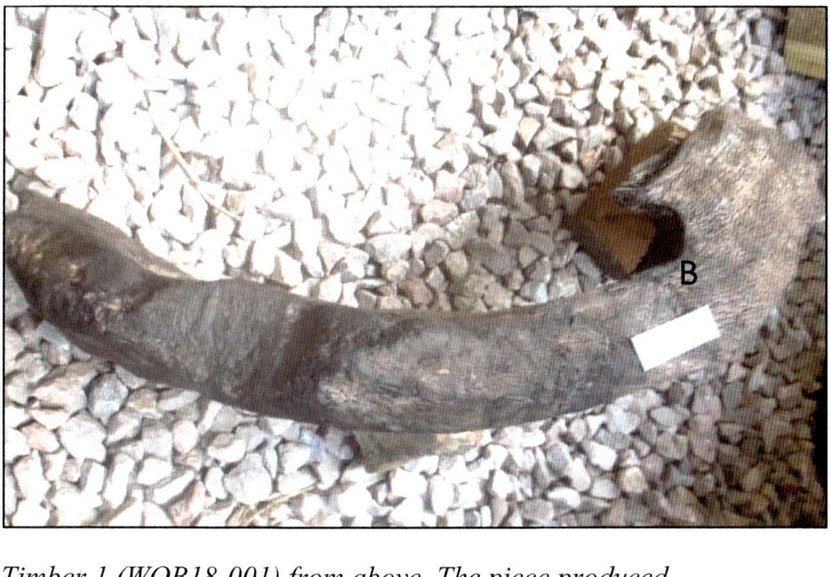

Timber 1 (WOB18-001) from above. The piece produced radiocarbon dates of 5106 BP + 29 years and 5160 ± 34 years BP.

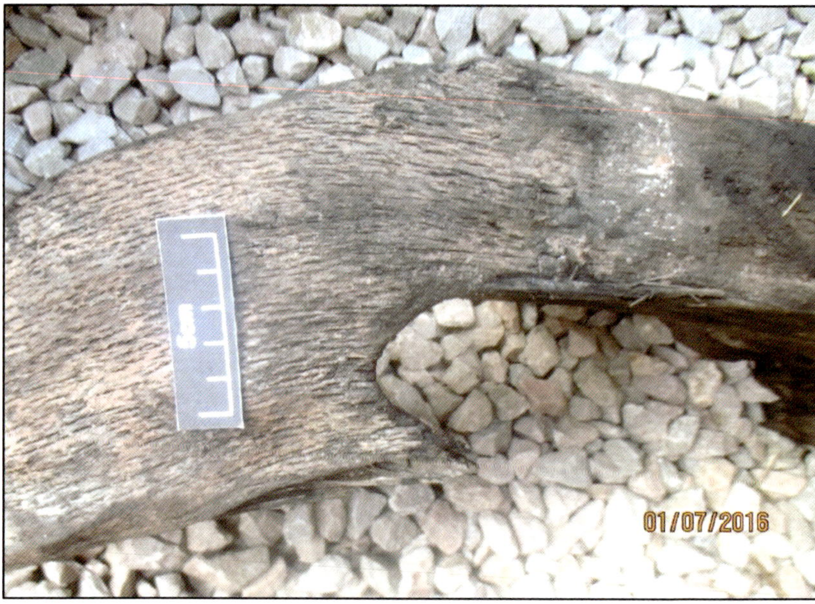

Timber 1 (WOB18-001) cut and worn feature from above.

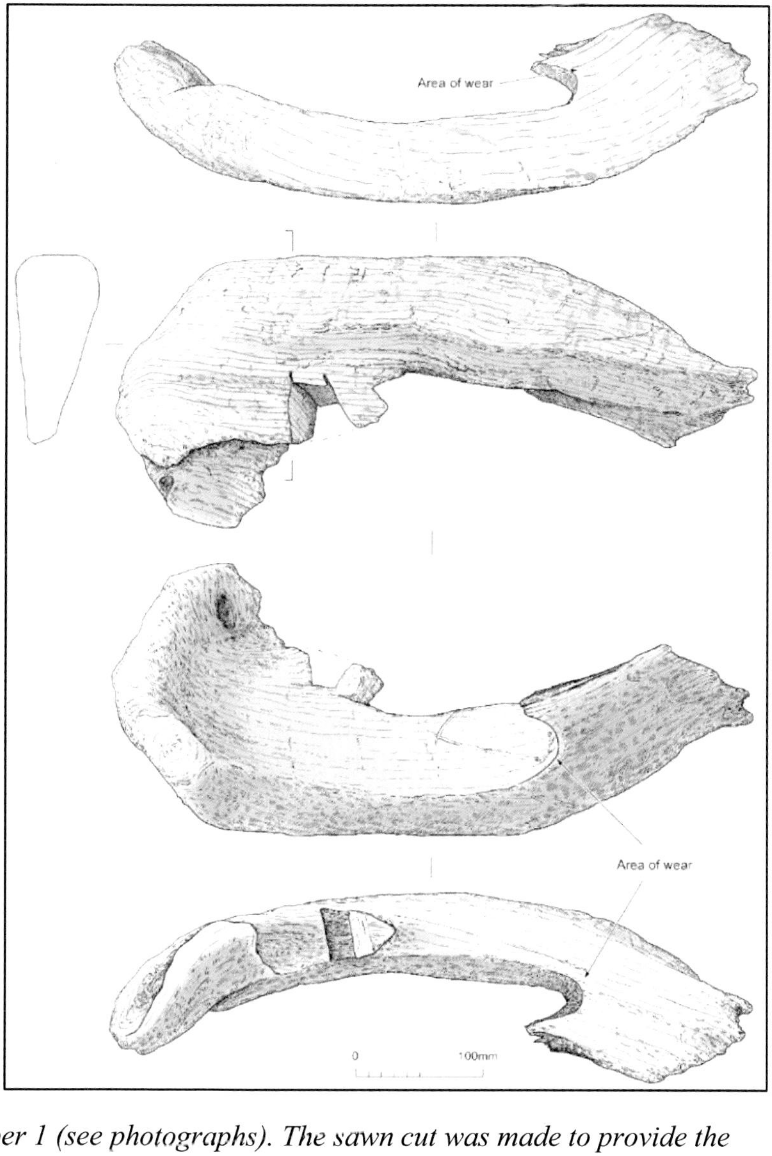

Timber 1 (see photographs). The sawn cut was made to provide the first sample for radiocarbon dating. WOB18-001: 5106 ± 29 years and 5160 ± 34 years BP. Drawings & some photographs – Ann Leaver

Worked timber 2 resembles part of the hull of a logboat; it has a large round hole, 7.5cm wide, cut through it horizontally where there are extensive signs of wear. If part of a boat, the feature may be associated with a rope or the attachment of another logboat or of an outrigger, or even to take an oar.
WOB18-002: 5071 ± 29 years before the present.

Worked timber 2 resembles part of the hull of a logboat; it has a large round hole, 7.5cm wide, cut through it horizontally where there are extensive signs of wear. If part of a boat, the feature may be associated with a rope or with the attachment of another logboat or of an outrigger or it may even have been to take an oar.
WOB18-002: 5071 ± 29 years before the present.

WOB18-003 (Timber 3): 5070 ± 29 before the present; WOB18-004 (Timber 4): 5082 ± 29 years BP. *Photo by Ann Leaver*

Criteria for logboat identification

THESE criteria were used by Professor Seán McGrail in deciding which artefacts of those he had investigated during his 1972-5 survey should be classified as logboats. Nevertheless, he said that it is possible that some entries in his catalogue are not logboats but other artefacts of similar form.

A hollowed-out fragment of wood is probably a logboat if it satisfied two or more of the following criteria:

The Monmouth Timbers are underlined:

(i)	It is found in or near a (former) watercourse *On the shore of the prehistoric lake*
(ii)	It is associated with other nautical artefacts: fishing-tackle, anchors, paddles, poles, etc. *None*
(iii)	At least one end is shaped in one of the well-documented logboat shapes *Gunwale and 'hull'?*
(iv)	Vestigial fittings normally associated with logboats ie, ribs, thwarts, tholes, stabilisers, etc. *Circular cuts, worn by ropes?*
(v)	It is greater than, say, 3m in length, *No*
(vi)	Bark and sapwood have been removed *Yes*

The Monmouth timbers seem to meet (i), (iii), (iv) and (vi).

However, Professor McGrail, on seeing the pieces, could not agree that they were definitely from a prehistoric boat, nor could he suggest what they might be. He could think of nothing in the literature like them but he did say that the worn hole in our suggested hull fragment was big enough to take an oar. Also if we could prove that all the pieces were from the same object it might strengthen our case for a boat. The abandonment of the timbers and their burning on the very edge of the lake appears to be significant.

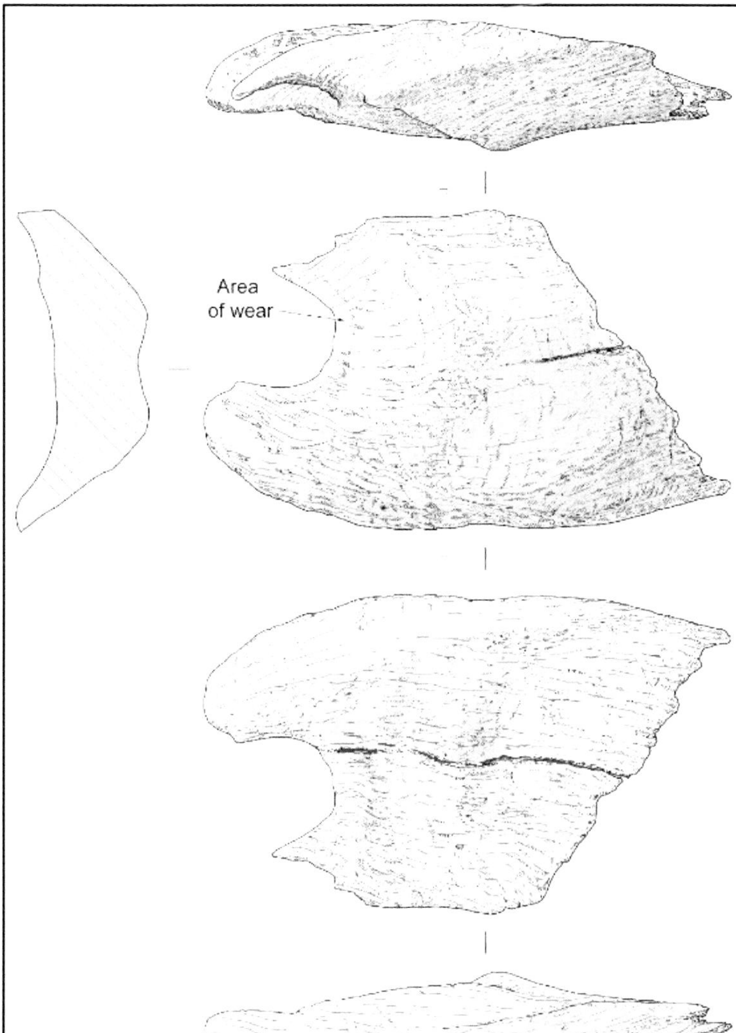

Worked timber 2 resembles part of the hull of a logboat; it has a large round hole 7.5cm wide, cut through it horizontally where there are extensive signs of wear. *Drawings by Anne Leaver*

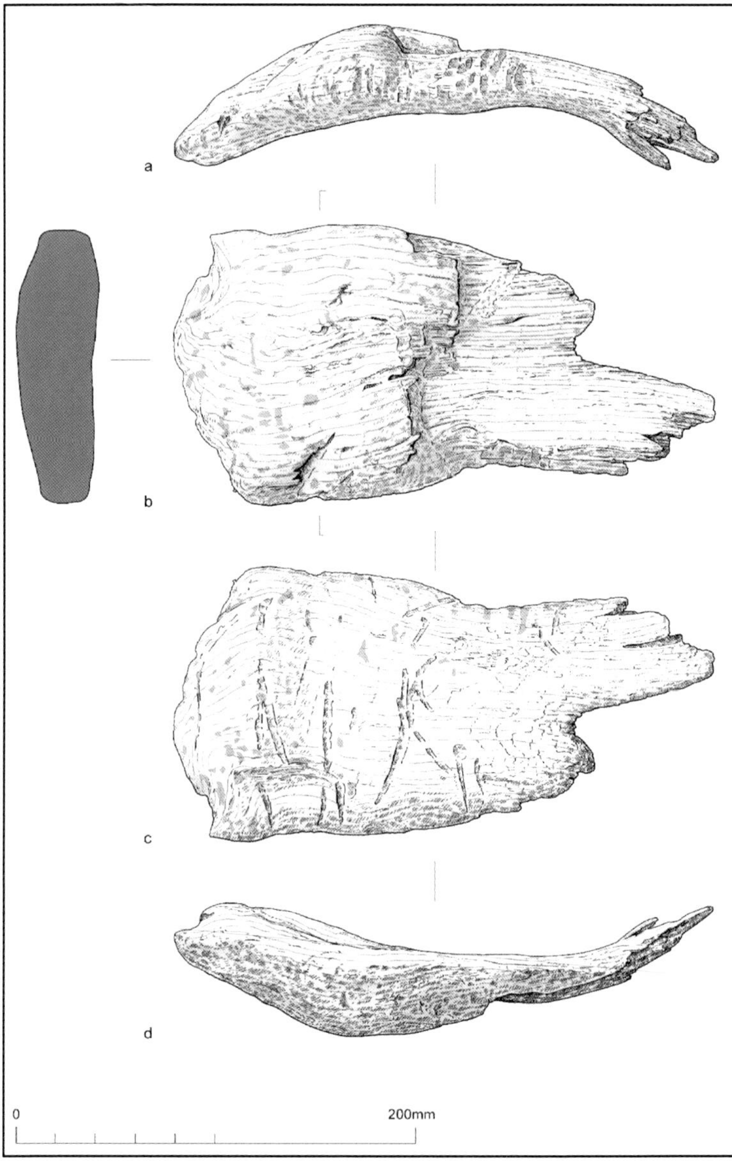

WOB18-003 (Timber 3): 5070 ± 29 years BP. Possibly a fragment of Timber 2. Drawings by Anne Leaver

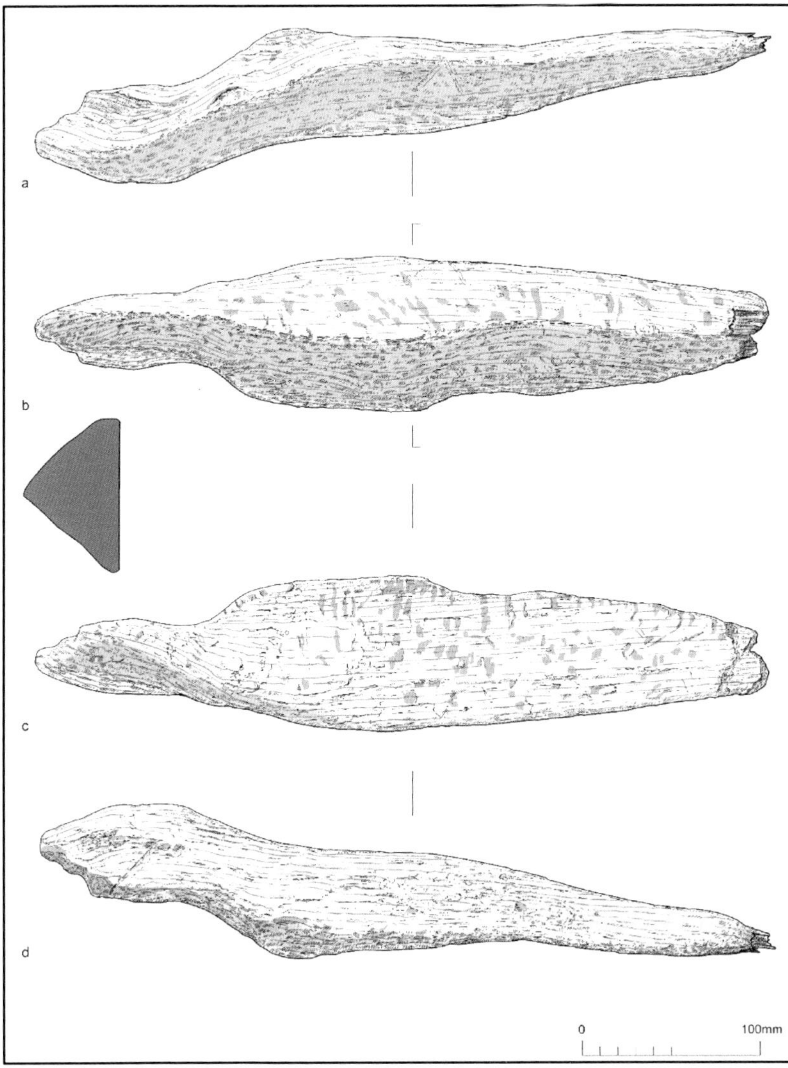

WOB18-004 (Timber 4): 5082 ± 29 years *BP.*
Drawings by Anne Leaver

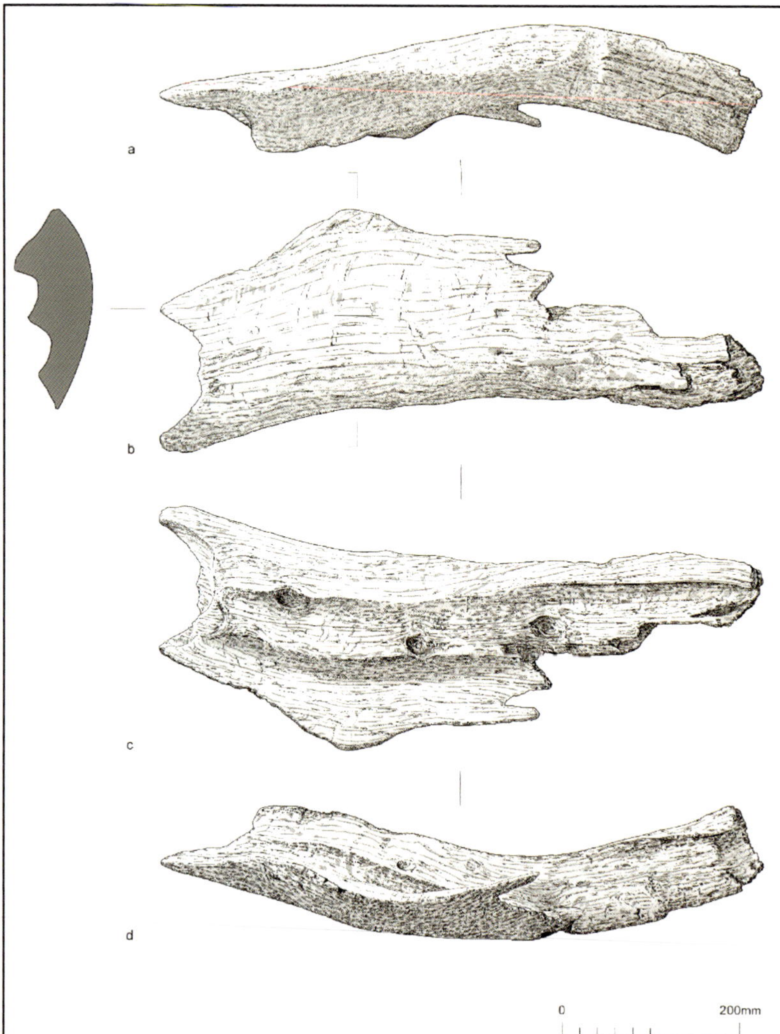

An unworked oak log recovered with the cut timbers

WOB19-005 (Timber 5): 5024 years BP ± 26 years.
Drawings by Anne Leaver

Ancient sailing boats.

I suggested in *The Lost Lake* that if more sophisticated prehistoric vessels other than log boats did exist they would be more likely to survive journeys across deep water and end up as firewood rather than being preserved in the mud of lakes and rivers like the many log boats found in Britain and Ireland. There is ample evidence of boats with outriggers such as those depicted in Bronze Age Scandinavian rock art and those with signs of fittings for outriggers or for the joining of two canoes, from Britain and Ireland, demonstrating the need for greater stability during crossing deep water. As Sir Barry Cunliffe says, in his 2001 *Facing The Ocean:* 'The archaeological evidence shows, with great clarity, that the sea lanes around the Atlantic coasts from Ireland to Shetland were in active use at least as early as the Neolithic period. Most of the traffic would have been short-haul and coastal but there is no reason to doubt that adventurers made more daring voyages' (p93).

Preserved wrecks must become rare with sophistication and time so I suggest that the cut and worn features on the 5,000-year-old timbers from the Monmouth Lake should be considered as possible evidence for much more complex boats in ancient times – even some with sails – as it seems unlikely that only Phoenicians were messing about in boats outside the Mediterranean.

Bronze Age potsherd 1000 – 800BC from Isles of Scilly - could be the earliest British depiction of a boat. Richard Moss - 22 Aug, 2012. On the right is a modern example of what it may have looked like.

A strange coincidence ?

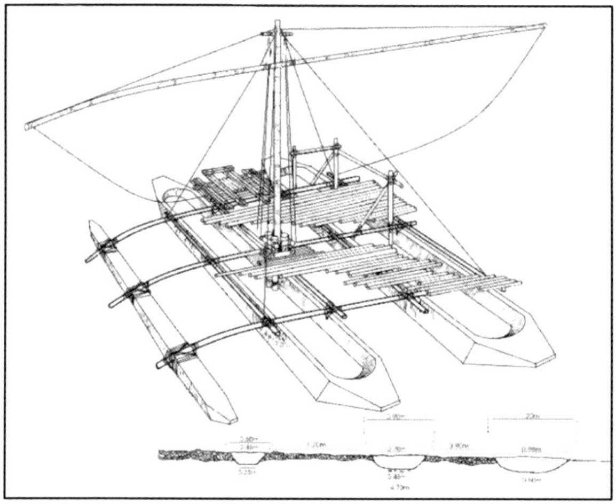

Peter Bere's reconstruction of a Parc Glyndŵr boat

FOLLOWING the discovery of the prehistoric channels on the lakeside at Parc Glyndŵr, Peter Bere produced an interpretation of the type of boat which may have been constructed on the site (*The Lost Lake,* Revisd Edition, 2016). Although kindly received in reviews in several leading journals the reconstruction did not please everone.

Our claim was that more sophisticated boats than simple logboats must have been used to cross to Ireland or to the Continent and that such vessels would be less likely to sink and be found preserved at the bottom of lakes or estuaries. They would be more likely to survive and later be used as spares or as firewood.

The discovery of the 5,000-year-old King's Wood Gate timbers, from beside the lake, with distinct gunwale and rope wear, has thrown the question of complex logboats back into the arena for the pieces do appear to match Peter Bere's reconstruction as well as Professor McGrail's Criteria for identyfying logoats. It had also been burnt, presumably where it had been landed on the lake shore.

Roman iron-working on the old lake bed

Archaeologists at work on the Roman site (far right).

The paved floor of the Roman iron-working site – apparently the first activity on the bed of the drained lake

The Roman pottery by Dr Peter Webster

Samian Ware from the iron-working floor

Roman pottery from the paved floor areas of the iron-working industry was examined by Dr. Peter Webster who reported:

Samian

- Form 29, South Gaul. A small portion of the lower zone of a bowl showing panel decoration divided by wavy line borders with a smudged rosette terminal. The panel to the left retains the legs of an animal. c.AD65-85.
- Form 37, Les Martres-de-Veyre. Only a basal wreath survives, framed by bead rows and consisting of repeated beaded circles, Rogers 1974, C24 (S&S, Fig.4, 3) used by Drusus 1 (cf. S&S, Pl.13, 160). c.AD100-120.
- Form 37, Central Gaul. Abraded panel decoration is divided by bead rows. Portions of three panels survive, from left to right: a small circle; the lower body of a man wearing a toga, O.911, over a very abraded ?mask; the scarf dancer, O343. The two figure types both appear in work signed by Albucius. c.AD145-170.

- Form 37, Central Gaul. A fragment from the base of the design which probably took the form of a winding scroll. A portion of a small vine leaf survives. Antonine.
- Form 33, Central Gaulish. A fragment of base, floor and wall. The form was made throughout the main period of Central Gaulish export, c.AD120-200, but was the most popular Antonine cup so an AD140-200 date is most likely.

Other Roman Pottery

All are from Context 003

- Curved rim jar in light grey fabric. The form was possibly as Manning 1993, Fig.110, type 28 (2nd-3rd century).
- Four fragments (including three joining rim sherds) of a small flask with 'pulley rim' in light red fabric and of a type generally termed an 'unguent flask'. The form is comparatively rare but widespread. Gillam illustrates the type from the northern military zone (Gillam 1970, type 38) and a not dissimilar flask was being made at Wilderspool (Hartley & Webster 1973, Fig.2, 7) although with a corrugated body which is absent from our vessel if the one body sherd belongs). The type also appears at Caerleon (Nash-Williams 1932, Fig.57, 122-3 with another complete but unpublished example from the western civil settlement). A fairly local source is likely for the Monmouth vessel. Most examples cited appear to be second century in date.
- Three sherds from the bases and lower walls of two large jars in Severn Valley Ware.
- Two rim sherds from a wide mouthed jar in Severn Valley Ware. The very plain rim (as opposed to a hooked rim) suggests a vessel such as Webster 1976, Fig.4, 21 and a 2nd century date.
- Eight sherds of a flanged bowl with slightly in-turned lip in Severn Valley Ware. Cf. Webster 1976, Fig.8, 46 (2nd-3rd centuries). Rawes 1982, Fig.6, 121 & 130 shows similar vessels with a handle which links them to a long-lived form of military origins (discussed by Greene in the context of vessels made at Usk, Manning 1993, 38-9 & Fig.6, 22).
- Flanged bowl, or more probably a dish, in Black-burnished ware, burnt light grey; cf. Gillam 1976, no.62 (mid 2nd century)

General Comments

The Wonastow Road pottery has suffered somewhat from soil action which has removed the surface, especially of the coarse pottery but is otherwise notable for the survival of multiple and often large pieces of individual pots, suggesting a discrete rubbish deposit rather than a redeposited midden moved by agricultural action.

There is one piece which is probably early to mid Flavian (the Samian form 29 fragment) but otherwise the collection is largely second century. There is a bias towards the middle 2nd century, but, it is more likely that the collection as a whole dates from the early to mid-2nd century. The preponderance of Severn Valley pieces emphasises the close links which the Monmouth area had ceramically with the Lower and Middle Severn in the Roman period.

The disastrous launching of the *Monmouth*, near Wye Bridge, 1825
By kind permission of Monmouth Museum

What happened to the Lake?

SEXTUS Julius Frontinus, the Roman general who set up the Fortress at Caerleon and subdued the Silures after AD74, is best known – apart from being a soldier – as an engineer specialising in waterworks. After sorting out the Roman war machine in Wales he went on to reorganise the water supply for Rome. And as Jane Bray has pointed out, it is thought that the Romans also successfully drained parts of the Gwent Levels and there should have been plenty of military labour to call on once the Silures had calmed down a bit.

The draining of the lake might have allowed ships to reach further inland and also revealed a large area of rich agricultural land to help feed the army – see the granaries in Usk. The site of the lake then became a very large fenland type of marsh where plant remains turned to peat and was followed by flooding and the accumulation of silt which turned to clay, sometimes under anaerobic conditions.

The archaeological evidence seems to be that the Romans were working on the bed of the lake shortly after it was drained, for iron slag and Roman pottery is regularly found in or close to the lake bed in and around the town. It seemed that the lake had survived into the Iron Age with dates of 2200 BP and 2281 BP, from wood and charcoal from the bed of the lake at Parc Glyndŵr; there was also Samian Ware from between the clay deposits filling the lake and a date of 2145 BP from the peat at Parc Glyndŵr which followed the reduction of the lake. However, a radiocarbon date from brushwood in the peat over the bed of the lake on the Barratt Homes site came out at 2221 BP. This may mean that the lake was reduced by that time or had become some sort of swamp which extended from Wonastow Road around to Parc Glyndŵr and a little beyond.

Crucial dating came from beneath the pebbly shore below the Roman horizon in St James' Street with a cooking pot sherd dating from around AD50. Equally significant were two radiocarbon dates from the same context: Charcoal 2020 BP and Charcoal 2120 BP and 1970 BP. There are lots of other instances in Monmouth of Roman contexts lying immediately over the bed of the lake or activities cutting holes into its surface. This is common in Monmouth with good examples being that of an early Roman iron-working site at Barratt Homes, Wonastow Road, below alluvial deposits with paleo-channels and the front defences of the Pre-Flavian Fort to the rear of 20 Monnow Street which must have been close to the edge of the lake (if we have the sequences correct).

Above: The front ditch of Monmouth's pre-Flavian Roman Fort to the rear of No 20 Monnow Street where the ditch protrudes into the flood plain. This should mean that the shore of the lake at that time would have been at least a little to the west of the ditch.

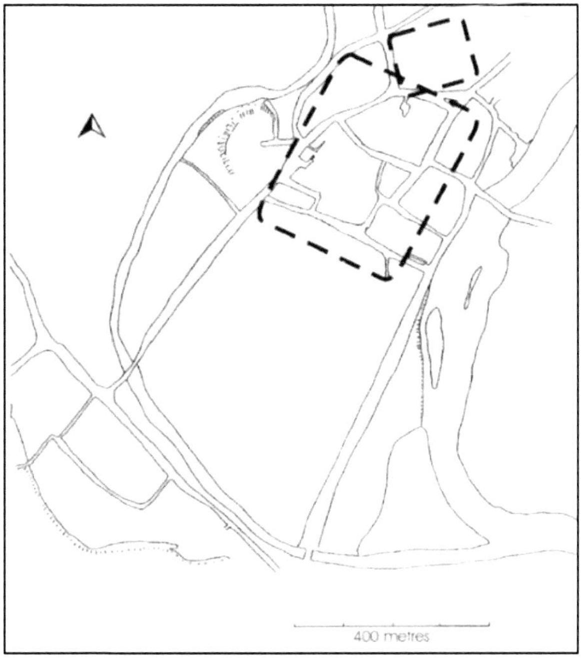

A plan of Monmouth's First-Century Roman Fort

Sextus Julius Frontinus was a famous general and a leading water engineer who sorted out Rome's water supply. He may have been responsible for draining the Monmouth Lake which would have allowed ships to reach far inland and create a large area of rich agricultural land – there were thousands of troops to feed. Frontinus may have also had a hand in draining the Severn Levels.

Ancient and Medieval floods in Monmouth

Prehistoric channels cutting a Bronze Age burnt mound

Commerce House, Monnow Street, Saxon and Norman house floors

22-24 Monnow Street flood silts (just below the centre of the section) archaeomagnetically dated to AD1315-1345.

During the tidal incursions of the Middle Ages which were recorded by Nennius and Geoffrey of Monmouth we should consider what was happening on the very slightly higher ground around the town – in Monnow Street for instance. There is ample evidence of severe flooding, especially during the appalling weather of the 14th century – a time of famine and the horrors of the Black Death. This tragic period is marked by collapsed houses and layers of silt in homes where the same local pottery was being used all over the town.

The thickest and the most impressive flood silt layers accumulated in lower Monnow Street where they must represent prolonged flooding and probably the evacuation and the abandonment of many houses where the road and even the sidewalks were covered in silt which has survived under the street and the pavements. In modern times, Monnow Street has always been flooded by the River Monnow, held back by high water in the River Wye which in turn must have been influenced by the tides in the Wye Valley.

There are flood deposits dated by pottery to the late 11th/early 12th centuries; the early 12th century; the late 13th/early 14th centuries; the 14th century and the 16th century. It is possible that the 13th century was relatively free of floods rather than that all the evidence has been destroyed. The 14th century silts which dominate the archaeological record mark the beginning of the end of the rising floors. This has put them in danger of disturbance during modern times so it is perhaps surprising that so many of them have survived. Most of the following sites contain undisturbed layers of silt with grain sizes measuring 0.02mm or less. The exceptions are at 95 Monnow Street (up to 0.2mm) which was away from the street frontage and possibly inside an outhouse; 1-3 Monnow Bridge (0.5mm) which was on the river bank. The first site recorded was 75 Monnow Street while a classic section was photographed by Monmouth archaeologists during a Cadw excavation (by GGAT) but no sample was taken by the archaeological contractors.

22-24 Monnow Street	AD1315-1345 at 60%
30 Monnow Street	–
35 Monnow Street	Early 14th Century
41 Monnow Street	–
43-47 Monnow Street	Early 14th Century
49 Monnow Street	Early 14th Century
61-63 Monnow Street	Early 14th Century
66-68 Monnow Street	Early 14th Century
69 Monnow Street	Late 13th/Early 14th Century
	12th Century
71 Monnow Street	Early 12th Century
	Late 11th/Early 12th Century
75 Monnow Street	Early 14th Century
83-85 Monnow Street	Early 14th Century
95 Monnow Street	Early 14th Century
No’s 1-3 Monnow Bridge	Early 14th Century

Further information and the grain sizes of these deposits are published in Appendix 1.4 of Flooding in Medieval Monnow Street’ in *Down the Dig*.

Monmouth Wye Bridge from Mayhill. These floods leave varying deposits of silt which are quite different to the layer of 'estuarine' clay left by the tides around the shores of the lake in Overmonnow. Could it be that sea levels had dropped after Geoffrey's time so that the tides did not again reach the lake? *Monmouth Museum*

The River Wye in flood. Looking towards the Quay – probably 1947

Undisturbed flood silts on 13th century surface of Monnow Street

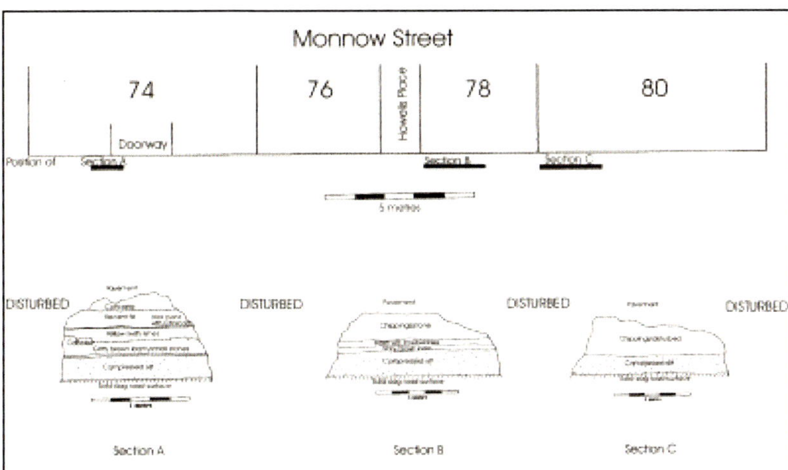

Section showing identical stratification of 14th century flood silts under the pavements outside 74 to 80 Monnow Street.
The same thick layer of silt covers the 13th century road surface.

Commerce House, Monnow Street, Monmouth – A 12th century house with evidence of Norman and some Saxon occupation. This 13th century phase, with pitched stone hearth, has been covered by 14th century flood silts.

Still water in Monnow Street *Monmouth Museum*

Appendix 1

Monmouth Priory – The Animal Remains

By Felicity Taylor

(Nids - unidentifiable fragments)

<u>Context 006</u>		
Bovine	24	Various, including teeth
Pig	14	Various, including teeth
Sheep	2	Tibia
Dog	2	Teeth
Nids	77	Fragments
<u>Context 009</u>		
Bird	15	Various
Pig	11	Various including burnt bone
Bovine	1	Pelvis fragment
Sheep	15	Various including 11 rib fragments
Fish	1	Vertebra
Small mammals:		
Rodent	1	Scapula
<u>Context 010</u>		
Sheep	2	Fragments
<u>Context 011</u>		
Pig	7	Various
Bovine	1	Rib fragment
Sheep	2	Various
Dog	2	Teeth
Nids	6	Fragments
<u>Context 012</u>		
Bovine	8	Various
Pig	17	Various, including teeth
Nids	21	Fragments
Bird	1	Humerus (Tawny Owl?)
<u>Context 013</u>		
Bovine	3	Various including dog chewed tibia
Pig	10	Various including tusk
Sheep	14	Various including burnt bone

Bird	2	Small and larger bird
Dog	4	Phalanges, front & back
Nids	34	Fragments
<u>Context 016</u>		
Bovine	1	Lower mandible & teeth
<u>Context 018</u>		
Bovine	3	Lower mandible and teeth
Pig	2	Humerus & phalange
Sheep	2	Rib fragments
Dog	3	Rib fragments
Nids	20	Fragments including burnt bone
<u>Context 021</u>		
Pig	4	Various
Nids	16	Fragments including 2 dog chewed fragments
Dog	2	Teeth
<u>Fill of drain cut</u>		
Lamb	2	Fragments
Pig	3	Various
Nids	8	Fragments
<u>In drain structure</u>		
Pig	1	Metatarsal
Bovine	1	Rib fragment
Nids	2	Fragments
Oyster shell	1	

Appendix 2

Monmouth – Notes from Gordon McDonald

Discussions with Gordon McDonald have been vital and an inspiration to me in my writing. Here are some of his important e-mails:

*As I understand it if Nennius lived circa 770 to 810 then that would have been towards the end of the Dark Age Climate Minimum. The tides never the less below Monmouth would still have been quite awesome, entering from the Severn Estuary and would amaze those that looked upon them. The tides progress up the Wye, also, unlike today, would not be impeded by the various bridges, field banks and modern day structures that choke the flow, which would have otherwise been up a broad estuarine tidal channel.

Geoffrey of Monmouth lived circa 1095 to 1155 in the middle of the Medieval Warm Period climate optimum so any account by him on the tides entering and leaving the Monmouth Basin (Llyn Lliwan) would be eye witness, contemporary, a first-hand account and therefore can be regarded as academically accurate.

A thousand years of human activity with farming reclaiming land close to and all along the course of the present day river channel has changed the nature of the Wye's valley out of all recognition to what it once was. Kind Regards, Gordon

*It might be useful to translate what 'Nennius saw'..... Nennius Historia Brittonum.

At the turn of the 8th 9th century AD the River Wye between Chepstow and Monmouth, unlike today would not have been impeded by various bridges field banks, enclosures and modern day structures choking its free flow. It would have been a broad estuarine tidal channel.

The sudden rising of every tide in the Severn Estuary at the confluence of the River Wye and the Severn would send a tidal surge up the Wye. This could continue unimpeded until it reached the Monmouth Basin (Llyn Lliwan) where it would mix with and hold back the outflow of the three rivers (Monnow Troddi and Wye). Back downstream the incoming tide would peak having left exposed (as Nennius witnessed) the bank/shore near the river. When the tide ebbed Lake Liuan (Lliwan) vomited all that it had devoured from the sea (and its three rivers) sending a surge of water back down river and in the process flooding the previously exposed riverbanks.

This is not what happens today for the reason stated in the first paragraph above but it is clearly what Nennius saw and recorded. It is possible that what he witnessed was a particularly extreme tide, but what is more likely is that this was a regular occurrence of the twice monthly high spring tides and then they behaved in a manner then which we are not familiar with today.

Kind Regards Gordon

Steve Clarke wrote: The medieval lake may have been restricted to the alluvium of the Overmonnow flood plain and this must have been filled to overflowing with the muddy (almost estuarine) water which was built up as slack water joined by water from the three rivers. The clay, which I've been calling anaerobic or alluvial, does extend out onto areas away from those parts filled with peat - 'dry' areas.

The alluvium would still have formed a fairly substantial lake but may have been the vestige of a far bigger post-glacial lake (overlooked by the hunter-gatherers of St James Street).

The bed of the original lake is composed of very compressed (or hard settled) rounded small pebbles and stones - in the main limestone, presumably from the hillsides of the White Hill where there are bands of the stone, together with an ancient kiln in 'Limekiln Wood'. This bed is where the housing foundation trenches are aimed at - sometimes six or more feet down. The depth of this distinctive hard bed varies considerably for it's almost immediately below the stone paving of the Roman ironworking site at King's Wood Gate but is covered by a metre or more of brown sandy loam further up the site. The lake village type of settlement under the two attenuation ponds is also just inches above the lake bed and so are the Roman 'vineyard' type of remains on the eastern end of the Barratt's attenuation pond. All of these remains were subsequently covered by thick layers of the clay / peat and clay. On the Bronze Age stilted settlement there was evidence of flooding leaving very fine silt.

There had been earlier alluvial deposits which were followed in large areas by the growth of peat. This, at Parc Glyndwr was preceded by a long period as a huge fresh water pond - with considerable pondweed marl over the lake bed. The absence of this pondweed lime marl on the King's Wood Gate area is unexplained unless the water there was too brackish or something as it was closer to the Wye and its tidal effects.

The huge lake suggested by our discoveries in St James' Street far exceeds the size of the lake which would have filled the lower areas of the

Overmonnow flood plain so perhaps the Llyn Lliwan of The Mabinogion was restricted to a lake from near Wonastow Road (the Siltbusters attenuation pond) to the Croft-y-Bwla side of Parc Glyndwr; on the west this would begin near the entrance to King's Wood Gate and continue east to at least Jordan Way. Still a pretty big lake: big enough to require a boat – perhaps one like that envisaged from the remains found near the King's Wood Gate site entrance

A thought. We were a bit concerned about how any prehistoric boats could get out of the lake to reach the open sea from Llyn Lliwan but this now seems not so much a problem if the slack water reached the lake a couple of times a day. Did they also use that to launch the big 19th century boats made in the town into the Wye below Wye Bridge?

* (1a) John Nettleship, by his biographer in *'A True Original – John Nettleship'* – in *Magick* magazine says: 'Elsewhere in the story Arthur and his men pursue the giant boar Twrch Trwyth from Ireland, across Wales towards the Severn, and meet up with him between Llyn Lliwan – *[vitally Nettleship leaves out Ewyas]* almost certainly the same as Llyn Liuan and probably the same lake as Llyn Llyw, since spelling was an inexact science at the time - and the mouth of the Wye. Because the names are given in that order - Llyn Lliwan, then the Wye - and they were coming from the west, the implication is that they came to Llyn Lliwan first, and it was both west of the Wye and close to it *[they were actually coming from the north]*. The mouth of the Wye lies just south *[east]* of Chepstow miles east up the Severn from Caldicot, therefore Llyn Liwan was either at or close to Caldicot. John himself preferred that name for it, "Llyn Liwan", presumably because it was the middle ground between Llyn Liuan and Llyn Llyw, as well as because Llyn Liwan or Lliwan is the version of the lake which was the most clearly located west of and close to the Wye.'

*Gordon McDonald notes:
An observation you might find useful to refer to in due course.
I have been reading John Nettleship's 'Caerwent Camelot and the magical coming and going lake'. He makes a well-researched and detailed case for the Nedern Brook tidal inlet as the location for Llyn Lliwan.

However, I don't think he realises that Nennius and Geoffrey of Monmouth were actual eye witnesses to the tides they recorded. Also the major flaw in John Nettleship's argument is simply 'Geoffrey of Monmouth and Caldicott Castle'. This castle is built close to the tidal inlet where the channel up to Caerwent narrows. In the early 12th century this waterway would be bustling with shipping coming and going as the construction of the castle commenced. There is no way anchored and docked ships of the time, with small boats unloading cargo and building materials survive the sort of tidal maelstrom these eye witnesses, in particular Geoffrey of Monmouth, described. *[see also Steve's comment that the hunt was coming from north to south, not west to east]*

Now of course the Wye river from Chepstow to Monmouth is crossed (and their abutments choke) by six railway bridges and four road bridges. So a broad estuarine channel now it is not. However, you have the dateable archaeological and geological evidence to prove the tides did wash into the Monmouth Basin 2,000 and 1,000 years ago making this 'Coming and going lake'. Hope you find this useful. Kind Regards, Gordon.

* The same thing happens on the River Severn, on the spring tides, when the river below Tewkesbury stops flowing and you get what is often called slack water. The peak of the tide in the river stops the natural flow, river water backs up and can rise a foot or so at Lower Lode. In one major flood event on the Severn at Gloucester, my crews were delivering meals on wheels (in boats) in Alney Terrace. The flood water was dropping slowly, then the tide came in and people who had just managed to start drying out their ground floors were flooded all over again. Kind Regards – Gordon

* Following on from yesterday's email I suppose the best way to answer your question is to look at it from a practical viewpoint, as a straight forward 'Risk Assessment' taking the likelihood of a tidal and a flood event as a percentage risk.

<u>Monmouth Basin Becoming Tidal</u>

By Year	Risk of Event
2020	4% risk/likelihood
2030	30% risk/likelihood
2040	60% risk/likelihood
2050	80% risk/likelihood
2060	95% risk/likelihood

As you say, the Planners have looked at the land on which houses are to be built in Monmouth as having a 1 in 1,000 year risk of a major flood event. I don't know how they have arrived at this assessment or what they have based this data on. However, what is clear is that Britain's climate has changed dramatically in the last 30 years with a concentration of warmer years and severe rainfall events....like this year in Yorkshire, Cumbria a couple of years ago and the Severn Valley flood of 2007.

The Severn Valley flood of 2007 was concentrated on the River Severn and River Avon catchment. It took out the Water treatment plant at Tewkesbury entered the Abbey and came within a whisker of taking out the electricity for the whole of north Gloucestershire. This was not an accident of Geography but an accident of chance in which the Wye and Usk valleys dodged the worst of the weather event. This randomness is impossible to predict but it does significantly alter the risk in certain locations like Monmouth where three rivers converge.

I therefore, in the light of the current climatic shift, assess the risk of a 2007 rainfall event occurring in the Wye, Monnow and Trothy catchment as follows...

By Year	Risk of Event
2020	20%
2030	40% - 50%
2040	80% - 90%
2050	90% - 100%
2060	100%

The risk of a major river or fluvial flood in the Monmouth Basin will be exacerbated by the progressive reach of the higher twice monthly Spring tides, particularly should this flood event occur around the lunar full or new moon. At low tide the River Wye drains past Chepstow into an empty estuary and the lower reach of the lunar Neap tides allows floodwater in the Wye to exit the river with reduced impediment. In the River Severn above Minsterworth there is the curious anomaly where the incoming tide is progressing up towards Gloucester but the actual level of water in the river is falling, the tide seemingly draining downhill inland? The Wye may do this as well but I am looking into it.

This is my best assessment at the moment. I am still looking at how the various bridges and their abutments affect the reach of the incoming tides and perhaps how these also affect the draining of floodwater from the Monmouth area. Kind Regards, Gordon

Old notice beside the Triwall sports field, off Wonastow Road

Parc Glyndwr attenuation pond during groundworks